BEYOND BODY LANGUAGE

Learn to read the hidden nuances of a smile, the seemingly casual placement of an arm. What do they mean in photos of your friends, your family, VIPs? Dr. Akeret's penetrating analysis of 230 photos will show you how to recognize and interpret the unconscious meanings of gestures, posture, expression.

Photoanalysis is an exciting new technique, a scientific method that gives you the power to discover from ordinary photographs what people really think about themselves and each other.

Included also is a special section on celebrities in the news, which shows how to interpret the power structure within the Kennedy family, the "two" faces of Richard Nixon, the sexuality of Marilyn Monroe.

The subject of nationwide interest and popular acclaim, PHOTOANALYSIS has been excerpted in *Ladies' Home Journal* and is an Alternate Selection of the Literary Guild.

PHOTOANALYSIS
was originally published by Peter H. Wyden, Inc.

*Are there paperbound books you want
but cannot find in your retail stores?*

You can get any title in print in **POCKET BOOK** editions. Simply send retail price, local sales tax, if any, plus 25¢ to cover mailing and handling costs to:

MAIL SERVICE DEPARTMENT
POCKET BOOKS • A Division of Simon & Schuster, Inc.
1 West 39th Street • New York, New York 10018

Please send check or money order. We cannot be responsible for cash. *Catalogue sent free on request.*

Titles in this series are also available at discounts in quantity lots for industrial or sales-promotional use. For details write our Special Projects Agency: The Benjamin Company, Inc., 485 Madison Avenue, New York, N.Y. 10022.

PHOTOANALYSIS

How to Interpret the
Hidden Psychological Meaning
of Personal and Public Photographs

by Dr. Robert U. Akeret
edited by Thomas Humber

PUBLISHED BY POCKET BOOKS NEW YORK

PHOTOANALYSIS

Peter H. Wyden edition published 1973

POCKET BOOK edition published April, 1975

The quote from Georg Groddeck, *The Book of The It*, translated by V. M. E. Collins, with an introduction by Lawrence Durrell, is used courtesy of Vision Press, London.

In some chapters of this book the names and identifying details have been carefully altered to assure the privacy of all concerned.

L

This POCKET BOOK edition includes every word contained in the original, higher-priced edition. It is printed from brand-new plates made from completely reset, clear, easy-to-read type. POCKET BOOK editions are published by POCKET BOOKS, a division of Simon & Schuster, Inc., 630 Fifth Avenue, New York, N.Y. 10020. Trademarks registered in the United States and other countries.

Standard Book Number: 671-78759-4.
Library of Congress Catalog Card Number: 73-86180.

This POCKET BOOK edition is published by arrangement with Peter H. Wyden, Inc./Publishers. Copyright, ©, 1973, by Dr. Robert U. Akeret and Thomas Humber. All rights reserved. This book, or portions thereof, may not be reproduced by any means without permission of the original publisher: Peter H. Wyden, Inc./Publishers, 750 Third Avenue, New York, N.Y. 10017.

Front cover photograph by Fred Samperi.

Printed in the U.S.A.

I wish to thank:
Ann Novotny for her photographic research
Winston Potter for his design
Frank Grunberg for his photographic assistance
Ann Klem for her help in shaping the book
and my publisher for suggesting it.
And all the families who allowed me to look
into their albums and use selected photos.

R. A.

CONTENTS

Picture Credits

The pictures reproduced here are used by courtesy of private individuals except for those in Chapters 10 and 11.

Pages 182: Bettmann Archive Inc.; 183: The Library of Congress Prints and Photographs Division; 184, 200, 204, 205, 208, 209, 212, 213, 218, 219, 226, 230-51, 259-71, 277-79, 284-303, 305, 306: United Press International; 185: Black Star; 187, 254, 281: Wide World; 190, 194: Cornell Capa/Magnum; 191, 308: Hiroji Kubota/Magnum; 192: Charles Gatewood/Magnum; 193: Eve Arnold/Magnum; 195: Leonard Freed/Magnum; 196: Charles Harbutt/Magnum; 197: David Seymour/Magnum; 198, 200: Sovfoto; 202: Arnold Newman; 206: Dennis Stock/Magnum; 207: Max Waldman; 199, 211: Marc Riboud/Magnum; 214: Time Inc., 1973; 216: Courtesy of Henry Luce III; 217: Burt Glinn/Magnum; 222-25: The Lyndon Baines Johnson Library, Austin, Texas; 229: Mike Lien/The New York Times; 253: Culver Pictures; 3, 4, 255: Bachrach/Photoreporters; 258: Courtesy of Senator George McGovern; 270: Eliot Elisofon, Life Magazine, Time Inc., 1972; 271: David Gahr; 272: From the film **Picasso,** a Rizzoli Film, distributed by Contemporary Films/McGraw-Hill;273-75: Robert Capa/Magnum; 278: Susan and Alan Raymond

Films, Inc.; 303: Henry Cartier-Bresson/Magnum;
304: Bill Stanton/Magnum; 307:
Courtesy of The Harry S. Truman Library,
Independence, Missouri; 309: Ken Heyman;
310: J. Delano/Library of Congress Prints and
Photographs Division.

I am not inviting you to follow me,
but to follow yourself.
I am only here to help if you need me.

—Lawrence Durrell's description of
Georg Groddeck in the introduction
to Groddeck's **The Book of The It**

PHOTOANALYSIS

How to Interpret the
Hidden Psychological Meaning
of Personal and Public Photographs

1.

Photos are mirrors with memories

In this country alone, millions of people take billions of photographs each year. Photos bulge from wallets, shoe boxes, and albums; fall from drawers and closets; clutter up desk tops and wall space; fill countless frames and slide projectors. Most of them are visual records of our families extending back through generations and including the most recent arrivals; many will be viewed and savored for years to come.

We know the joy of sitting together after a family vacation and viewing projected slides or looking at printed photos. Reliving the recent trip brings us closer together, and often there is a flash of recognition when we discover a photo that is particularly telling, poignant, or humorous, especially when it has caught someone unaware in an unusual mood or position. But even though we take them, collect them, and show them, what do we *really* see in all these photographs? Do we ever go beyond superficial responses to analyze the tremendous wealth of information that is stored in them? Can we use these photos to learn something deeper about ourselves?

And what about the countless photos taken by professionals that illustrate newspapers, magazines, and books? How closely do we look at them? What can they tell us about the people and events they depict?

After many years of using family photographs in my psychoanalytic practice, I am convinced that most of us are visually illiterate and we miss completely the valuable, rich, documented sources of personal and interpersonal information that is caught and fixed in photographs. Most people rarely look at photos beyond a fleeting glance; they don't linger with these precious records or reexamine the familiar. And they are not attuned, motivated, or disciplined to mine them for what they are worth. And yet, as Oliver Wendell Holmes noted years ago, photographs are like mirrors with memories. They document our personal developmental past, reminding us where we have been and how we have developed. Also, they graphically illustrate for us the attitudes and emotions of people in public life or in newsworthy situations whom we will probably never know or see in person.

Let's see how you can discover some of these hidden meanings yourself by looking at some examples.

The first photo is of the Kennedy family, taken in Hyannis Port in 1934. From left to right are Joseph, Jr., Eunice, Rose, Robert, John, Edward, Joseph, Sr., Kathleen, Patricia, Rosemary, and Jean. It's a remarkable shot, a study in family unity of one of America's greatest political dynasties. It's a close family, a happy family, by any standards a rather attractive family. But what else can we see here? Are we missing a crucial, hidden element if we just look at it and dismiss it so quickly? Let's look at it again, this time with the help of some extra lines drawn in to call your attention to the family grouping.

Now. Look at how central and close the boys are to their parents, and how peripheral the girls are. We all know how the Kennedy men were pushed by their parents and what they became. Here we can actually see the emphasis that the Kennedys placed on the male children and the way the children acted out parental expectations.

A significant measure of any child's importance or value is reflected in his parents' attitude toward him. And even if we knew nothing about the Kennedy family, this photo makes quite clear that the boys are all important, while the girls—although seemingly not unhappy—are relegated to lesser positions in their relationships with their parents and in their parents' expectations for them.

There are further aspects to the Kennedy photo that I'll go into in a later chapter. We'll also make some candid appraisals of other famous people as revealed in photographs: Richard Nixon, FDR (in a photo that offers some additional insights into his now revealed relationship with his secretary, Missy LeHand), Marilyn Monroe, Picasso, and the British Royal Family, to cite just a few.

But right now, let's look at a photo that would never see light in a newspaper, a photo similar to the ones we all have in our own photo albums.

What do *you* see in it?

Like most people, you probably see a father, his son, and his daughter. Given the background and their informal dress, you guess they are on a vacation in the country. They seem cozy, affectionate. They stand close together, and the father warmly and protectively has his arms around the children. They are all relaxed, casual.

In addition, you may remark that the photo is interesting, dull or nice, a good or bad shot, or offer any of several dozen other qualitative clichés that are normally used to categorize most photos. It's just another family snapshot, you say, and you've got any number of similar ones you can show me.

If that's your reaction, take a further, longer look. This seemingly innocent, everyday photograph—certainly it was casually taken—is packed with meaning, some of it disturbing and mystifying. There is an element here that shouldn't be, something unusual and out of character with the other elements.

Give up? Then look at it with me.

The daughter is tilting her head slightly toward her father, indicating a closeness with and an affection for him. But she is having trouble making the contact. There is an obstruction, something preventing her from getting closer. If you look closely you will see it is her brother's fist. His arm is extended straight and stiff behind his father's back, and his fist pushes against his sister's neck.

When I first saw this photo, I asked the daughter, now in her thirties, if she and her brother had fought. They had, constantly, for many years, but she could not understand how I knew, since she had never mentioned it.

"It's all there in the photo," I said. As we talked further about her relationship with her brother, she realized that the fist in the photo was symbolic of their battles, and of the anger and resentment her brother had expressed toward her since her birth, when she displaced him as the only child. As he used the straight arm and fist in the photo to keep her away from her father, the brother often used the same technique to keep her away from him. He would infuriate her by teasing, and then hold her off so she couldn't move in close to retaliate.

But even though she had lived through it, and had looked at the photo hundreds of times, she always saw only what she had been conditioned to see: an ordinary, happy family. Now she had been awakened to new elements.

When we started looking at it together, she was deeply impressed by the fact of her own visual blindness, and felt that looking at photos would never be the same again; a new respect had been awakened in her for the potential hidden meaning in typical family snapshots. Her "awakening" was not just idle talk, either; I could see it in operation as she approached other photos with greater anticipation and increased perception.

Those are just two examples of what I'm trying to demonstrate. Photographs have a special language of their own, and *all* photographs tell some kind of story beyond the purely visual record. Obviously, not all photographs are equally rich, and many tell more when viewed as a series rather than singly. I don't wish to imply that by analyzing photographs we can tell everything there is to know about someone's personality or his relationship with others. People are infinitely complex and multidimensional. But, like dreams, body language, slips of the tongue, and handwriting, photographs reveal significant aspects of individuals and are lasting records of our lives and deeds. From them we can accumulate significant and valid knowledge about ourselves and others—knowledge that is frequently beyond external observation or otherwise obscured.

Think for a moment. The human face is capable of displaying thousands of different expressions, each of which has something to say about us, about how we react to the world around us. Photography can capture every one of those expressions, whether we intend it to do so or not. And a photo offers a pure visual experience that is not contaminated, distorted, influenced, or distracted by words or movement. You can go over a photograph time and time again, and every time you look at it—if you know how—you can discover new meanings, new experiences, new sensations.

I call the study of photographs to arrive at personal and interpersonal insight photoanalysis. It is a psychologically sound method of increasing self-awareness, and, as the first photos have illustrated, it can help anyone become visually sensitive to the nuances of personality and interpersonal relationships that are recorded in photographs.

As will be demonstrated throughout this book, it is a

discipline with specific guidelines and workable techniques; but it is a skill that can be learned by anyone. Extra tools are not necessary; keen eyes are. It is, in approach, no different from acquiring any other skill such as interpreting dreams or learning how to read. It is neither witchdoctoring nor an exact science. There are boundaries and limits, and the principles offered in this book are meant to be suggestive rather than definitive. (For this purpose, all the photographs selected and analyzed deal with people.) And there is risk, because it takes risk to become involved in increasing self-awareness and self-understanding. But photoanalysis can be an illuminating, rewarding, even creative experience, and it can open new, or perhaps just unused, doors in our search for a more complete understanding of ourselves and of our relations with others.

2.

Discovering the hidden story behind the picture

Sam was a bright, industrous, outgoing college student. To talk with him casually, you would not get the impression that anything was wrong. But in fact Sam was locked in a destructive relationship with his mother. As a psychological counselor at City College of New York at the time, I had been seeing Sam for several months. Because of the excessive demand for help and our limited staff, Sam and I were only able to work together for thirty minutes once a week.

It is, of course, not unusual for teen-agers and adults to have occasional fantasies and dreams about sexual experiences with parents. But Sam was obsessed with the idea, and his mother was openly encouraging his attention by acting seductively around him. Fearing he might lose control and actually make overt sexual advances toward her, Sam was on the edge of panic. I was alarmed because nothing I did or said was making any headway in resolving the crisis. We needed some kind of leverage to explode his obsession.

For some reason, more intuitive than calculated, I asked Sam to bring me some photos of his mother. At our next session, he hesitantly handed me one.

"What's so sexy about her?" I asked after looking at it for several seconds. The middle-aged, overweight woman in the picture obviously made little effort to keep herself attractive. There was nothing remotely sensual or erotic about her.

Sam looked crushed, but I pressed on. "Tell me. What is so erotic about her? Take a *good* look." I thrust the photo back in his hand and waited for a response. He stared at the picture for several minutes, as if it were the first time he had ever really taken a good look at his mother. Unable now to rationally defend his sexual interest, he finally admitted, "I've been reacting to her advances. I never stopped to think what she's really like."

That was exactly what we needed; the photo produced the leverage to begin breaking the sexual tie. Sam had been so engrossed in the sexual titillation of his obsession that he had never taken a cold, detached look at his mother, nor had he considered the consequences of acting out his fantasies. Seeing and accepting his mother's harsh sexual reality was the beginning of a healthy relationship with her.

Alan wished he had been born into another family. He was having more than the usual amount of difficulty in making the transition from his low socioeconomic background to being a highly regarded and talented engineering student. Deeply ashamed of his past, he felt he would never be able to escape his childhood background—the semi-slum neighborhood, the dirty apartment house he grew up in, the way his immigrant parents thought and talked. He felt contaminated by it all, and was sure that anyone could see through his exterior to his true past. He did not take girlfriends home to meet his parents, and many of his dreams and fantasies emphasized how unsuccessfully he was attempting to separate himself from his past.

In one session I asked him to come with his parents,

but he declined, rationalizing that the experience would be too upsetting for them. I asked him to bring some photos, but he said none existed. Then I stressed that anything that would clarify or give additional information about his relationship with his parents and his past might help him work through his shame. Several weeks later, quite unexpectedly, he brought some torn and well-worn photos.

"I was wrong," Alan confessed, "my mother found these stored in an old hat box."

His parents had been stunned by his request—Alan and his parents had not communicated personally in years—and Alan had been equally stunned when his mother had actually searched for and found the photos.

The first photo Alan showed me was of his grandfather standing in front of a new church door with magnificent hand-wrought iron hinges. From the expression on his face, you might have thought that he had built the church singlehandedly. He was, however, the town blacksmith in a rural Russian village; he was known for his skill in designing and making door and gate hinges. The pride of his life was the rebuilding of the church, which had been severely damaged by fire. In his face Alan and I easily recognized his feeling of accomplishment, and I also detected a slight sense of pride in Alan's tone as he retold the tale to me.

There were other photos that had special meaning for Alan—especially one of his mother's parents, who had worked on an aristocratic estate in Russia. That photo showed the grandparents standing beside a formal garden, which they were responsible for maintaining. Their faces were stoic; they looked a hundred years old, yet they were not bent or humbled by their work in the soil. Again I noticed a growing sense of pride in Alan's description of them and their work.

When Alan had picked up the photos, his parents began to talk for the first time he recalled about their lives, how they met, why they decided to emigrate to America, and their struggle to carve out a small business, a hardware store in New York.

Alan and I both knew that a significant and fresh change had occurred in his sense of his past. He had experienced feelings of pride, especially for his grandparents, that he had never felt before. He had learned something new about his origins. The visual experience of the photographs had helped to start the change, as it had broken the stranglehold that shame held on Alan's developmental past.

Joanne was finishing her senior year, majoring in psychology. In spite of her training and better-than-average awareness and understanding of herself, she could not remember much of her childhood between the ages of ten and thirteen. It was as if she were blocking out the years around puberty. In addition, her fear of death was unusually overwhelming.

Working with Joanne, I frequently wondered if she had experienced some painful trauma during that time which had led to massive guilt feelings. That could account for her loss of memory. As to her fear of death, I was inclined to suspect that perhaps a parent or other authority figure (she was Catholic) had warned her that behavior of some type (possibly sexual) would lead her straight to hell.

Joanne and I tried working on the problems through associations and dreams, but because of the limited time available, we were making little progress. Hoping they might stimulate her memory, I asked her to bring in some family photos.

Though she tensed at the idea, she could not verbalize why. She arrived at the next session with a family album, but remarked that she hadn't gone through it beforehand. We were looking at it together when I was struck that there seemed to be more members in her family than she had ever mentioned. There was a boy, younger than she, whom I had never heard her talk about.

"Who is that?" I asked.

Joanne's face took on a strange, tormented look. She appeared to be fighting desperately to remain in control of herself, to hold back a flood of tears. Rather than try to calm her, I encouraged her to cry, even scream if necessary.

The tears flowed freely for several minutes before she collected herself and began to speak. The boy in the photos was a younger brother. When Joanne was ten, her family discovered that he had bone cancer, but refused to have him hospitalized. Joanne's mother and aunt took care of him in the home, and when she was old enough, Joanne helped. As the story poured from her, she recalled the odors when she changed the sheets, the pain of feeding him meals, and his slow and agonized decay. When Joanne was thirteen, her brother died.

For years the experience had been too painful for her to remember. By blocking it out completely, she had been able to deny that it even happened, but she had not been able to repress the fear that she might also die. The photo activated a memory that was almost unbearable for her, but one that she had to recapture if we were to work through her fear of death.

As she left, I asked Joanne to leave her family album. We had concentrated on one photo, but there were others that might be useful in tapping her emotional resources and happier memories. During one of our next sessions we opened the album and followed her family through a month's summer vacation in Israel when she was nine years old. The photos were typical of a family vacationing. There were shots of them standing in front of the Wailing Wall in Jerusalem, and picking fruit on a kibbutz. And there was another photo of Joanne's younger brother; he and she were splashing playfully and vigorously at each other in a pool. That photo didn't upset her; it had been a happy time for them together.

Joanne then recalled some of the events of the trip, and especially the fun her family had experienced in looking at the photos afterward. Her father had made a happy event out of it, telling appropriate vignettes from the trip about each family member. After relating this, Joanne softly commented, more to herself than to me,

"I want a family with many, many children."

I was touched and pleased, for if Joanne was not afraid to have children for fear that they might die, then she was well on the road to resolving her fears about her own death.

My work with Sam, Alan, and Joanne took place when I was just beginning my professional career, and offered my first glimpses into the potential of using personal photographs in psychoanalysis. But my personal fascination with photos had far earlier roots.

My mother always treasured her extensive collection of photos—of her grandparents, her parents, her growing up in a large Swiss family, her career, her marriage, my childhood and development. As a youngster, I looked at them frequently, questioning my mother in great detail about the identity and personal characteristics of the people in the pictures.

Although I could not have been consciously aware of the implications at the time, I am now sure that the degree of my interest was directly related to the fact that my parents divorced when I was very young. Living with my mother, I was constantly on the move—from Switzerland to America, to eight different schools in my first eight years of formal education, from temporary home to temporary home. I was without roots, without a father, without the reinforcement of belonging—that secure feeling that frequent contact with close relatives provides. As compensation, I used the family photos to attain a sense of continuity in an otherwise disrupted life.

There were some photos that I treasured particularly: the photo of my parents' wedding day in which they posed at a bridge over the Rhine; my mother dressed in her formal wedding gown and my father proudly beside her; the surrounding flower girls and accompanying wedding party. They looked so happy with each other then. I was also fascinated by a series of photos of my own growing up in Switzerland, especially those with my parents still together. Then there were later photos of me

in a T.B. sanatorium and in a *Kinderheim*. My past
was all before me, to be carried along with me
in photos wherever I happened to be.

Years later, while I was undergoing analysis, I found
that I had no memory of any physical contact with
my mother. I avoided her physically but admired her from
a distance. I didn't dislike her, but contact was clearly
threatening for some reason, and I assumed the feeling
had also existed throughout my childhood.

Trying to document or disprove my memories, I
began to dig through old photos, finally coming upon
one taken of me when I was seven years old, on an
Easter-egg hunt. There I was, beaming with delight,
sitting in the grass surrounded by the colorful eggs I'd
found. Close beside me, with her arm warmly around
my shoulders, was my mother, as happy as I was.
The photo was spontaneous and reflected the joy of
the hunt as well as our closeness.

By looking at the picture, I was able to correct a
distortion in my memory that had made a lasting, and
damaging, impression. Discovery of this fresh
photographic evidence forced me to reconsider the
origins and causes of my difficulties in relating
physically with my mother.

I had suspected that my reluctance to be physically
close with her had its origins in the trauma of my parents'
divorce or my T.B. hospitalization, when my mother left
me alone for months. But I had no conscious memory of
either experience; I was too young. Now I had visual
proof that the difficulty started later, after I was seven,
and I realized that the cause could be linked with our
coming to America, when I was eight, and leaving father,
relatives, and friends behind—which proved to be a
valuable insight.

Since my initial, exploratory work with Sam, Alan, and
Joanne, I have continued to develop, refine, and use
photoanalysis in my private practice over a period of
almost twenty years. The results of that work have led me

to the conclusion that all photographs of people have some kind of psychological story to tell.

I have seen hundreds of people and worked with thousands of photographs on countless roads of discovery. The more I worked, the easier it became for me to recognize and explore important themes. As my experience increased, I could validate my impressions by asking questions about what I saw in the photos. Through analytic work in previous sessions, I had some sense of people's past experiences and could check out the reality of significant themes by using the photos.

In my present work, as part of any initial consultation, I may ask if the person has any personal family photos with him; most people—myself included—carry particularly meaningful photos in their wallets or handbags. If someone does, I suggest that we take a look at them to see what we can learn. Then, depending on the photos, I begin to ask questions and make relevant observations: "Does your father always look so depressed?" or "No one seems to touch anyone" or "Your parents look very pleased with you."

If the photo is recent and shows a relationship, I may ask, "Does the photo reflect typical feelings you have for another person?" or, if appropriate, "What a beautiful family you have. Tell me about each member." While seeking answers, I am also encouraging the person to ask his own questions and make his own observations about the photos.

Later, I specifically ask that photos be brought. Hopefully, many of them will be informal, spontaneous shots that capture the developmental stages of the person growing up in his family. At this point, new themes frequently surface and old problems are seen in a new light.

Some of my work with photoanalysis, while always requiring a fine sense of visual perception and a knowledge of exactly what to look for, has proven to be no more than the application of common sense coupled with sound psychological principles, which will be discussed in following chapters. But the results have been consequential. Other parts of my work, utilizing more innovative techniques and requiring deeper insights, have provided some startling results. All of my work in the area has convinced me that photoanalysis can be an exciting and extremely useful tool in deepening our understanding of ourselves and others. This is true whether it is used in conjunction with therapy or simply as another means of improving and broadening our visual perceptions of the people whose photos we see in newspapers, books, or magazines, as well as those close to us.

Over the years, I have tried to find other published research about the use of photographs in psychotherapy, but surprisingly little has been written. Some of my colleagues at the William Alanson White Institute have made informal presentations, but I know of no systematic study on the use of photos in psychotherapeutic encounter. There is, however, a growing literature that focuses on non-verbal communication which has relevance to photoanalysis.

In his seminal book, *Non-Verbal Communication,* Jurgen Ruesch points to photographs as powerful examples of non-verbal communication and states that photography is capable of recording most of the emotional and action expressions of an individual. And Dr. Ray Birdwhistell, a professor at the Annenberg School of Communications at the University of Pennsylvania and one of the pioneers of the science of kinesics (body language), says, "We learn our looks, we're not born with them."

Obviously, Dr. Birdwhistell is not contradicting the fact that we are born with certain features or inherited characteristics. He is saying that *experience* determines how those features develop and change, how our inner feelings about ourselves and others affect outer expression. The way we shape our mouths, the height of our eyebrows, our posture, whether we generally look depressed, joyful, angry—these and other similar aspects of our looks are, within genetic limits, learned responses. Additional studies by Dr. Birdwhistell have shown that couples who have been married for many years begin to look alike. Their lives are so closely entwined, their activities and emotions so similar, that they tend to react as and look like a unit rather than two separate individuals. Obviously, there is no better way to document the findings of Drs. Ruesch and Birdwhistell than through photoanalysis.

We know that body language works, that voluntary as well as involuntary expressions of movement, posture, etc., can accurately reflect the inner feelings and motivations of people. Words can lie, but—with extremely rare exceptions—the body does not. The validity of the lie detector offers a prime example of the fact that the body transmits messages we cannot control.

Some skeptics sneer at the suggestion that photographs can be psychologically revealing. "What can you tell about a photograph?" they demand to know. "Photos are posed. Most people being photographed just follow directions. They are told to smile and where to stand and how to position their bodies. So what can you tell from that?" A surprising amount, as we will be seeing later in this book.

Not all photographs are posed, and a great number reflect freely and naturally expressed spontaneity. Many have been taken without the subjects' even knowing they were being photographed. From them, we can make exactly the same determinations we could make if the camera were not present. In fact, we can make much more detailed observations because the camera has frozen the movement, thus allowing us time for adequate analysis and appraisal.

But what of the skeptics' specific objections? Even if a photo has been posed, it will still tell a significant story. People are not mechanical robots; they react to virtually nothing with computer precision and consistency. Every individual responds to any directive in his own unique way. So what if the photographer demands a smile? First of all, there are some people who just won't smile, no matter what. Others will smile, perhaps apologetically. But it is not the *fact* that someone smiled in response to the photographer that is crucial to us, but *how* he smiled. We could get: the plastic smile, the fake smile, the compliant smile, the empty smile, the provocative smile, the mystifying smile, the joyous smile, the clowning smile, the leering smile, the sneering smile, the hostile smile, the bored smile, the lover's smile, the partial smile, the full smile, the anxious smile, or a lot of other smiles. The particular smile will determine the quality of the story we are able to tell, but we will certainly be able to tell some story. Posing can affect it, but cannot completely control it.

In the next chapter I will demonstrate how anyone can learn and use photoanalysis; first, let me indicate its wide-ranging and exciting potential through some examples. While these examples come from my analytic practice, and involve people trying to solve specific and crucial problems, their application can have as much significance for people in general, not just those specifically in analysis.

Photoanalysis can help determine the reality of present and past experiences, and can aid the individual in a more precise and accurate recollection of those experiences.

Maxine's mother had not wanted to be pregnant, and Maxine's birth had been prolonged and difficult. Her mother showed little interest in her, believing she was ugly and useless because she was a girl. Clearly, her mother valued only boys, and that contributed to Maxine's becoming a tomboy.

Two frequent events throughout her childhood made Maxine despise and hate her mother. One was the regular beatings that her mother inflicted on her when she was "bad or sexy." During the spankings, they would lock horns in a battle of wills, mother trying to get her to break, to cry, and Maxine fantasizing "the ringing of bells" to take her mind off the pain. Maxine never broke, but she always wanted to vomit when her mother insisted on a kiss after the beatings. Then she would cry her guts out in her room.

The other hateful event was her mother telling her something only to later deny what she had said: "Why, Maxine, I never said such a thing! How could you think that of me?" She did this so often that Maxine could no longer trust her own perceptions. What did go on? Had her mother said or done what she remembered? Or was she imagining it? She didn't know. What I knew, though, was that her mother's ploy was an extremely effective way to drive someone mad.

Maxine had always sensed that since she met her husband her mother valued him more than she valued Maxine. And when Maxine's son was born, her mother gave the child the kind of loving, total attention that Maxine had never experienced. Whenever her mother came for a visit, Maxine felt an emerging, competitive "ownership" battle for her son. Who would feed him? Who would read to him? Play with him? Change him? Dress him? Hold him in family photos?

Many young mothers would more than welcome parental help and involvement, but Maxine distrusted her mother's motives, believing she was determined to undermine Maxine's loving relationship with her son. Although Maxine coped with her mother's attempts at behavioral domination, she could not confront her verbally. In her mind, Maxine kept hearing her mother's old familiar retorts: "Why, Maxine, how could you think that of me? Do you really think I would do such things? What's wrong with your mind?"

One session after a visit with her mother, Maxine was quite shaky. "It's happening again, Akeret. I don't know what's real anymore. Am I imagining my mother just doesn't give a shit about me? She waltzed through the door Sunday and breezed right by me—gave Peter [Maxine's husband] a clutchy hello hug—and then picked up Adam [Maxine's son] and walked off to play. I swear to you, she didn't for a moment acknowledge my presence, and it went on like that all day. Or did it? That's what's driving me crazy . . . am I imagining all this or is it real? Does she want Adam all to herself? Don't I count at all?"

I had a stack of photos in the office that Maxine had brought a few months earlier. We had looked at all of them and picked a few. There was one particular photo of Maxine with her son, both relaxing playfully on the floor. I saw such spontaneity, such trust and joy in both faces, that I challenged Maxine's fear that she might be doing to Adam what her mother had done to her.

"Where's the evidence in this photo?" I had pressed.

But we both knew there was none. Such fears had some basis in fact, but for the most part her communication with Adam was free from distortion and destructive exchanges. The photo was visual proof that their experiences together were generally positive.

Now I suggested we take another look. We came across another photo, taken by Peter, of Maxine's mother, Maxine, and Adam.

"Look at this one," Maxine exclaimed. "There we are—the happy threesome. All smiles. We appear so happy together." Then Maxine began to laugh, almost hysterically at first. The laugh turned to recognition, and finally to relief.

"Look at Adam. He's in the middle, being held by us both, and look *how* he's being held." I see clearly what Maxine has caught—the power struggle going on in the photo. Her mother had her hands firmly around Adam's lower legs, and Maxine had gripped Adam's waist. Each had her smile for the camera, but each also had a firm, unyielding grip on the child. Who would get him? If each had pulled vigorously, Adam would have torn apart across his middle.

I could see why Maxine was so relieved. There it was for all to see: Her mother's participation was not imaginary, it was real. She was an active rival, competing with Maxine for Adam. The photo reinforced Maxine's own perceptions, validated her experience, and supported the fact that, despite what her mother had always said to the contrary, Maxine had a firm grip on reality.

As a result of the photo experience, Maxine's self-esteem grew, and she felt less "crazy," far less vulnerable to her mother's rejecting behavior. As her mother became less confusing to Maxine, she also lost some of her destructive power. The experience eventually helped Maxine separate from her mother, and consequently to develop the necessary trust in her own observations and sense of personal value.

Photoanalysis can correct distortions in an individual's life experience.

Alexi seemed to care more for his dead mother than for his living wife. In his words, his mother had lived only to nurture him and provide for his needs. Alexi's idea of marriage was that his wife should do the same—that she should be bound to him in a relationship in which he was everything to her, but she only of limited consequence to him. He thought of her as personal property, and felt that she must, like all women, be kept "well down and in place."

Alexi had originally come for help because of overreaction to his mother's death. He had completely lost emotional control, screaming out for her and becoming overwhelmed with guilt. She had given him so much, but had left him before he had time to repay her. She had also committed the unforgivable crime of deserting him in midstream, while he still needed her. "She could have at least lived until I died," he told me in one of our first sessions.

That Alexi had no deep sense of self-worth was clear from his insatiable need for adoration and special attention. He lived in the past, trying to resurrect his mother through his wife, who was being destroyed by his efforts to establish and implement his concept of marriage. Despite dreams with such themes as "an elderly woman being boiled in a cauldron," Alexi could not bear to face the reality that he harbored unconscious murderous feelings toward his mother. After all, she had loved him totally, without reservation. Or had she? Something didn't quite fit; if his mother was so adoring as Alexi would have me believe, then why were his conscious and unconscious feelings about her so different? I asked him to bring some early family photos of them together.

"I couldn't find many," Alexi commented when he returned several sessions later with a half-dozen pictures, "but here's one where my mother is holding me in her arms when I was a baby. Doesn't she look at me adoringly? Look at her loving eyes."

Alexi was submitting his evidence, beaming with satisfaction. My eyes traveled from his face to the photo; I was shocked. His mother was holding him all right, but she looked depressed, totally uninterested in her son.

"Where's the adoring look you see . . . and those loving eyes?" I challenged.

"Right there on her face . . . there," he countered, but not very convincingly.

"Where?" I snapped. "All I see is an unhappy, burdened woman." Finally Alexi saw what I saw; no matter what his fantasy needs told him, he could not deny what the photograph had captured, and documented.

The reality of the photo forced Alexi to challenge his compulsive, conscious belief that his mother had loved him blindly. Here was an example where he was not loved, where he was experienced more as a burden than as a treasure. This started a reevaluation of his entire developmental experience with his mother, and I knew that once he saw the reality (both the positive and the destructive experiences with her), he might begin caring more for his living wife than for his dead mother.

23

Photoanalysis can activate those psychological resources of an individual that are beyond awareness.

Debbie felt the "light had gone out" inside her. When she came to see me, she was indifference personified. Nothing stimulated her, and even her seven-year marriage had ceased to be nourishing. Her parents had recently died prematurely and unexpectedly, and it seemed as if Debbie had almost died with them. She was experiencing no feelings, neither pain nor joy, and was able to harness only the energy required for simple daily maintenance. Whatever life there was within her was released through physical symptoms such as stomach cramps and prolonged headaches.

When her husband left her for another woman, Debbie's indifference and apathy turned to shock, depression, and then panic. "How will I survive?" she asked. "Everyone is leaving me. I've never been alone in my life." That her husband had rejected her for someone else activated a deep sense of despair about her own worth. She knew she had failed in providing her share of support for the marriage, but still his leaving hurt deeply.

The crisis, however, was at least making her feel again, and even though her feelings were disturbing and painful, her life energy was returning; there was some hope for personal change. This hope became realized as she started to tap and express her anger toward her husband.

As we worked to clarify her past personal history and to search for reasons why her "light had gone out," I asked her to bring any family photos she had. I was looking for a pattern, a developmental record of change that could visually document her loss of feeling. When she brought them, I was delighted to find a long series from the earliest years of her life to the present.

In the earliest ones, Debbie's sense of life and vitality was most impressive, and there was no evidence of depression or apathy. As we looked at them together, Debbie studied one particular photo for some time, as if it had a very special message to offer. The contrast between the bubbling two-year-old in the photo and the mature woman beside me was startling. In the picture she was bursting with joy, brimming with spontaneous, happy feelings.

"That's me," she said, somewhat disbelieving. "I haven't looked like that in a long time." She was not upset, as I had anticipated. Instead she said, "I'm going to have that photo enlarged, as big as life if possible, and I'm going to hang it conspicuously where I can't miss it, where it will follow me around my apartment. I want it in the open—to remind me of what I was, and can be again."

Debbie's will to live was evidently returning; the photo had sparked memories of when she was happy, memories long since "lost," and had ignited a desire for change.

Photoanalysis can pinpoint times of dramatic changes in looks, physical appearances, and feelings.

Susanne was shy and introverted, and being with other people terrified her. But this had not always been true. Originally from the Midwest, she was alone in New York, working as a teacher. Although she was intelligent, well-educated, and extremely well-spoken, she had no close friends outside her work, and openly discouraged any kind of sustained relationships. "I don't know why," she told me, in a way that made me feel that she was not *that* unaware. "I get invited out; I want to go, but at the last minute I always come up with an excuse why I can't. Soon the invitations stop. I guess I'm just very uncomfortable in social situations, and it's less frustrating for me if I avoid them."

Although not unattractive, Susanne was conspicuously overweight, and it took no great analytic mind to see that her size had a great deal to do with her problems. But we needed specific details if we were to make progress, some tangible developmental history from her about the weight problem, and she was reluctant to discuss the topic.

I asked for a series of photographs, and she brought in many. Those taken when she was a child and in her early teens featured a radiant, svelte young girl, fashionably dressed, and a sure candidate for cheerleader, majorette, or prom queen. From ages fourteen through sixteen, many of the photos were of her and a handsome boyfriend in a variety of teen-age activities. Not a few of them featured the couple in bathing suits.

At age sixteen, however, Susanne began to change dramatically, gaining weight, wearing dresses that hid rather than emphasized her body. The radiance was disappearing, and one could see bitterness and contempt in her face. In contrast to earlier photos, which always featured her in the foreground, the later ones showed her almost trying to hide behind other people. Where she had once been the center of attention, she was now virtually ignored. And there were no further photos of her boyfriend.

As we talked about the photos and the changes I saw, Susanne told me that as she became larger and larger, her boyfriend had deserted her for a shapelier girl; her other friends seemed to disappear. She retreated deeper into herself, substituting intellectual development for social activity, moving to New York, where she could remain anonymous, rather than stay in her home town, where her size obviously meant there was something wrong with her.

I asked her specifically what had happened at age sixteen that made her gain weight so rapidly, since none of the earlier photos had indicated any weight problems. In a burst of anger totally unlike her, she answered, "Because he wanted to fuck me." Then she began to cry freely, and told me how painful that sixteenth year had been because her boyfriend had pressured her to have sexual intercourse and she had become hopelessly deadlocked in indecision—wanting to and yet terrified. Her unconscious solution was to gain weight. The more she gained, the faster her boyfriend made his exit.

I was relieved—at last she was facing the weight issue—but I pressed on. "Why were you so terrified of sex?" I asked. Her tears returned as she related how a town drunk had attempted to rape her right after puberty. The experience, which she had never told anyone about, had thoroughly disgusted her; so every time her boyfriend attempted to have intercourse, the vision and memory of the nightmarish experience with the drunk flooded her mind.

Thanks to her photos, we were making progress with the weight problem. The photos pinpointed when she gained the weight and the fact that it was a sudden physical change. They also provided the impetus for us to begin dealing with the problem rather than avoiding it. She began to diet, and as she lost weight, she regained her social confidence, and was soon dating again.

Photoanalysis can be extremely useful in uncovering the subtleties and complexities of an individual's relationship with other people.

Jessica felt that her relationships with men had been a series of failures and that marriage, which she so desperately wanted, might elude her entirely. Everything about her was remarkably constrained, and while her body was trim and well-developed and her clothes obviously expensive, she was always overdressed, as if she were making a conscious effort *not* to look attractive.

Jessica's mother had died when Jessica was four, a loss from which Jessica never recovered fully. The youngest of eight children, Jessica always felt like the runt of the litter. She was socially isolated, awkward, alone. She never trusted her own abilities. And while her father's vicious temper was seldom vented on her, she dreaded it; he could turn on her at any moment. If Jessica approached him for emotional support, his answers were curt, dismissing her problems as insignificant.

27

When Jessica was in her teens, her father, preoccupied with his virility, remarried. Jessica's stepmother was young, beautiful, flamboyant, and overwhelming—certainly no mother figure for the young girl, who was already having enough troubles emerging. Verbally, however, her stepmother pushed Jessica toward a glamorous career. "Become a celebrity!" "Knock 'em dead!" "Wow 'em!" were everyday slogans. Despite the verbal encouragement, I was suspicious of the stepmother's aspirations for Jessica. Jessica and I both realized that her stepmother might well be serving her own needs for celebrity status rather than honestly encouraging Jessica to be outgoing, but there was still something missing in Jessica's understanding of their relationship.

While going over some family photographs one day, we noticed one of an anniversary celebration that included Jessica's immediate family as well as some other distinguished guests. We had not previously paid much attention to the photo, but now Jessica lingered, her eyes scanning the faces as if searching for something. She finally focused on herself.

"I was starting college at the time. I . . . I look awful," she started. "I'm all buttoned up with endless buttons, and that dumpy suit—it's hanging on my body. I look just awful . . . matronly. The suit hides my figure. You wouldn't know I even had a figure. What am I doing looking like that?"

Jessica was silent for some time. She continued to look at the photo. Then she said, "Look at my older sisters. They look attractive in their dresses. And my stepmother—she looks sensational." Jessica then started to laugh, but there was considerable anger behind the laughter.

"You can certainly see *her* figure all right," I said, referring to her stepmother. "How does the contrast make you feel?"

"Pretty damn mad. *She* knew how to dress. What was *I* doing in that horrible suit? Why wouldn't she help me?

28

Advise me? How could I wow anyone looking like that? Now I'm wondering what she *really* wanted for me. To be a glamorous celebrity or a failure?"

Jessica was on the right track. Her stepmother's behavior had become less elusive and less mystifying. The photo caused Jessica to actively question her stepmother's motives, to see the discrepancy between what her stepmother said and how she actually behaved.

Later in the session, Jessica and I looked again at a photo of her real mother holding Jessica when she was three years old. It was one of the last photos taken of her mother before her death a year later. In it, Jessica was being lovingly held by her mother, who was sitting in lush grass under a flowering tree. Jessica had no conscious memory of the experience, but looking at the photo provided a most moving experience. There could be no doubt that her mother had loved her deeply, without reservation. It was written in her eyes and in the way she supported Jessica in her arms. And the setting was so peaceful, so abundant, and so exclusive with just the two of them together. That photo made Jessica feel very special and loved, and the contrast with the other photo jolted her into a realization of her stepmother's true motives.

Those examples illustrate some of the major areas in which photoanalysis can prove useful—either in discovering resources or in clarifying the roots of difficulties in living. There are, however, certain limitations to photoanalysis. People are too complex to be completely captured on film, and while photos can reflect significant aspects of personality and interpersonal relationships, they can't tell everything. What we detect in photographs is behavior, and while the experience behind that behavior can be indicated, it cannot be fully determined without validation.

Photos can only suggest the future, not predict it. Photos can't tell whether a person will remain the same or change, but a series of photos will record the process

29

of change. Photos cannot reveal whether what we see is the key to someone's personality or relationships or whether it is momentary and fleeting. In that respect, facial expressions generally tend to be more momentary experiences, while body posture tends to indicate more fixed attitudes and moods.

The more we know, however, about the photographs and the people in them, the more useful and accurate photoanalysis is.

3.

How you can learn photoanalysis

Minor White, the professor who established the creative-photography program at MIT, has written that "the audience can be as creative as the photographer." That is true, whether we are viewing photography as art or considering the potential of photoanalysis. In either case, the audience must be willing to make the effort, and respond with heightened awareness.

   The key to learning photoanalysis is to shift from standardized response to a deeper, more personalized expression. Let's say we meet an old friend on the street. One of our first sentences will almost surely be: "How are you?" That is a standardized response to a standardized social situation. Most of us expect the friend to answer, "Fine." If he does, then we don't have to extend ourselves further. But what if the friend verbally indicates his well-being, and yet has a large bandage on his head or looks particularly depressed? Or what if he says he's been quite ill? Now we are compelled to question him further and to express more personalized, more specific feelings. With photoanalysis, the standardized response will not suffice at any point. We must always take the initiative; we must extend our perceptive powers as far as they will go; we must use our imaginations; and we must adhere to realistic guidelines. Use your perceptions, but do not overuse them. Check them out—not in the spirit of inquisition but as a journey of self-discovery—by seeking whatever factual information you may not have concerning photos by talking with others involved in the photo. Do not jump to conclusions you cannot support.

Every photograph is the result of a complex relationship among photographer, subject, setting, and culture. Only rarely are we able to accumulate unlimited information about each, but the more hard, factual knowledge we have, then the more accurate and useful photoanalysis becomes.

Ralph Hattersley, one of photography's most provocative writers, has observed that "when we look at a photo, we're also looking indirectly at the person who made it." The photo reflects the maker just as a painting makes a statement about the painter. And no two photographs are alike, because the photographers will reflect and express both conscious and unconscious aspects of themselves. If we told ten different photographers to photograph a woman on a hill, we would get ten distinctly different pictures.

Each would include what we requested: a woman and a hill. But the possibilities for variation are almost endless. Each photographer could choose different women and different hills. The ages, appearances, dress, and moods of the women could be widely divergent. We could get photographs shot at different times during the day, in different weather, and at different angles. Some might be formally posed, others casual.

Since the impact of the photographer can be so powerful, the first step of photoanalysis is to establish the nature and extent of his participation. We should know who the photographer is, what his relationship to those being photographed is. Is he father or mother, husband or wife, friend or stranger, amateur or professional?

We should know something about his style and approach to taking photos. Does he direct, telling people where to group, how to look? Or does he allow the photo session to develop naturally and spontaneously? Does he coerce? Order? Does he assault, using the camera as a weapon, intruding where he is not wanted? Does he have permission to take the photo? Do his subjects even know they are being photographed?

We should know something about his personality, about his needs, feelings, and special interest as he takes the photo. If he is angry, for example, his anger may influence the feelings of his subjects. We should know something about his feelings toward those he is photographing. And we should know something about his reactions to taking photographs in general as well as at the moment he took the photograph.

The subjects of photographs are, of course, our prime concern in photoanalysis. From them, we are seeking exactly the same kind of information that we would be if we were trying to make psychological observations from personal contact. But the photographic image has the advantage of being frozen. Since it will not change or move, we can analyze it at length and in depth. It can't and won't lie—although it may hide. What we see determines what meanings we are able to extract. But we must be careful that we do not distort what we see.

Let's say we have a photograph of an older woman with a bowed or hunched figure. Looking for psychological meaning, we might guess that she's trying to hide her breasts for some reason, or suggest that she is in some kind of emotional pain. But she could also have arthritis, simply be exhausted, or perhaps the camera just caught her in mid-stoop as she bent to pick something up. If we cannot be reasonably sure of our perceptions, then assumptions are out.

We must also determine whether what we see in a photograph can be reliably attributed to the subject's personality or his usual interaction with others, or whether he is reacting to the circumstances of having his picture taken.

The setting—the actual events surrounding the taking of the photograph—is important to know for photoanalysis; it affects what happens during the photographic session and, thereby, what we perceive.

Jurgen Ruesch, in his *Non-Verbal Communication,* believes that gesture and movement are a function of the cultural communication system of which an individual is a part. He writes: "Gesture among Americans is largely oriented toward activity; among the Italians it serves the purpose of illustration and display; among the Jews it is a device of emphasis; among the Germans it specifies both attitude and commitment; and among the French it is an expression of style and containment."

We know that Italians practice passionate emotional expression and that the French display style in their gestures and actions. But America is a country made up of many different national and racial strains, even regional influences—so there is no single typical cultural behavioral pattern. The gestures and behavior in photos will reflect the particular setting one grew up in, most likely a blending of more than one culture, race, and region. In analyzing photos it is important to bear in mind the specific social and cultural background of the individuals in the photos.

To a great extent, what is experienced and seen in a photo is determined by the interpreter's background, interests, and expectations. A professional photographer may focus on the composition of the photo and the quality of the print. A medical doctor might notice and even diagnose a physical disability. A psychoanalyst will undoubtedly look for personality characteristics and interpersonal relationships. Your attitude toward analyzing a photo is important, too, because if your expectation is narrow or limited, then little beyond the surface will be perceived, and nothing new will be learned. But if you are curious and open to the possibility of learning, then photographs become rich resources of new insights.

The actual procedure of photoanalysis is basically one of careful observation, of asking and answering the right questions. The right questions stimulate your eye contact and search, and—regardless of your prior orientation—the right questions, those that are resourceful, relevant, and provocative, govern the information you obtain.

The following questions and instructions are suggestive; they are by no means complete. They are offered to stimulate your perceptions, to demonstrate the wide range of possible experiences while analyzing a photo, and to give you a basic idea of the step-by-step process of photoanalysis you can apply to any photograph.

What is your immediate impression? Who and what do you see?

What is happening in the photo?

Is the background against which the photo was taken of any significance, either real or symbolic?

What feelings does it evoke in you?

What do you notice about physical intimacy or distance?

Are people touching physically? How are they touching?

How do the people in the photo feel about their bodies? Are they using their bodies to show them off? To hide behind? To be seductive? Are they proud of their bodies? Ashamed?

What do you notice about the emotional state of each person? Is he: shy, compliant, aloof, proud, fearful, mad, suspicious, introspective, superior, confused, happy, anxious, angry, weak, pained, suffering, bright, curious, sexy, distant, blank, bored, rigid, arrogant, content, lonely, trusting, strong, crazy, involved, frustrated, attractive, docile, bemused, correct, friendly, hurt, spontaneous, satisfied, depressed?

Can you visualize how those emotions are expressed by facial dynamics and body movement?

If there is more than one person in the photo, what do you notice about the group mood—the gestalt of the group? Is there harmony or chaos? How do the people relate? Are they tense or relaxed? What are their messages toward each other? Who has the power? The grace? Do you see love present?

What do you notice about the various parts of each person? Look carefully at the general body posture, and then the hands, the legs, the arms, the face, the eyes, the mouth. What does each part tell you? Are the parts harmonious or are there inconsistencies?

Pay particular attention to the face, always the most expressive part of a person.

Learn to read any photo as you would read a book, from left to right, then downward. Go over it again and again, each time trying to pick up something you have missed.

Ask yourself more general questions, as many as you can think of.

What is obvious and what is subtle?

Where is the sense of movement? (Or, is there any?)

What memories and experiences does the photo stir in you?

How do you identify with the people in the photo? How are you alike? How different?

What moves you most about the photo? What do you find distasteful about it? Is there anything that disturbs you?

Try to define the social and economic class of the people photographed. What is their cultural background?

If it is a family, would you want to be a member of it? Would you want your children to play with theirs?

If the photos are personal—of you, your family, friends, or associates—try to remember the exact circumstances of the photo session.

How have you changed since then? How have you remained the same?

The list could be endless, but these questions give you some idea of the approach photoanalysis must take. As we begin to work with actual photographic examples, you will see that it is not really difficult at all. It means keeping your eyes open for new discoveries. It can add adventure to your daily life as you become aware of the implications in the media and in the books you read.

The best way to learn photoanalysis is through example and actual experience. Let's take the photograph on page 39 and analyze it together, step by step.

Study it carefully for a few minutes. Now look away from it and see how much you remember. How many people are in it? What are they doing?

Now look again. What are your first impressions? What feelings are evoked in you? Describe to yourself what you see.

I am immediately impressed by the sense of life and vitality that radiates from this happy family. The photo pulsates with energy and spontaneity. In fact, there is so much energy on the part of the children that the parents need to exert considerable effort to keep them contained for the photo session.

Now let's move to more specific observations. The family is large; young parents with their four children. The children are all pre-school age, and there appears to be about a year's difference in the ages of each. Since this is a contemporary photograph in an age of birth control and family planning, four children so close in age could indicate religious beliefs prohibiting birth control, or accidents. I don't think so, however; the body attitudes and facial expressions of the parents give every indication that these children were planned. They are definitely wanted. Each child already seems different in personality.

This is a physically oriented family. People touch one another, but the touching is expressed from the parents toward the children; the children do not touch each other.

The parents relate more through their children than with each other. The father is with his daughters, the mother with her sons.

It is a family that obviously enjoys doing things together. The father is present, which I have found to be rare in most family photos. Usually the father (occasionally, but not frequently, the mother) is the one who takes the photos. But here is a complete family that is not locked in a stiff, formal studio shot.

The family seems as open and free with the photographer as they are with each other. He has photographed them freely and naturally, not in the rigid poses so often imposed by studio photographers. Their rapport with him suggests that he is a close family friend. This reinforces my idea that he is a talented amateur rather than a bored professional.

Now look at each individual in the photo. Look at the person first as a whole, then focus on the legs, body, arms, hands, and face. Pay close attention to the mouth and eyes. Which eyes draw you? Are there any that disturb you? Do you feel comfortable with all members of the family?

The father is a handsome, vital man. He is alert, sensual, very much alive, and he enjoys his children. He covers a lot of ground, his hands touching three of the four children. Physical touch is not hard for him. His energy is directed at keeping the children together for the photo session. His mouth is formed almost as if he is giving a verbal command: "Okay, everyone . . . stay together . . . stop squirming." Or perhaps he's singing or humming for everyone's amusement. It is obvious that he's the leader, the director of the photo session, and he has talents as an entertainer.

He has no eye contact with any other family member, yet he is not posing or looking into the camera. He could be self-centered, into his own narcissistic presence, but I doubt this, because of his physical relatedness with the others. I am more inclined to believe that he couldn't make a choice of whom to focus on because that would necessitate showing a preference for one member of the family over the others. By default, he is looking into space—but still is very much in control. I sense that this man has many interests and talents, and there is almost a magical quality in his personal magnetism—we are automatically drawn to him.

The mother is an attractive, outgoing, joyous woman. Her smile is full and genuine; it is not just plastered on for the occasion. She is thoroughly enjoying the session and her family. She leans into the family. Her body is turned into the center, and her legs are turned in the direction of the family center. She holds her youngest son, and she doesn't need to cover as much ground with the children through touch as her husband does. She, too, relates more through the children than with her spouse. She and he do not touch at all, even though their opportunities for doing so are ample. Their bodies could have touched at the shoulders, or their hands could have touched in their efforts to contain the younger son.

She is a vital, sensitive mother who has borne her children well and is completely able to cope with them. She has also kept her figure and her appearance. I have the feeling that she values individuality and self-expression.

The older daughter is at that shy, awkward, self-conscious stage. She is sweet, coy, happy, and very feminine. She stands in the middle of the family, acting almost as a bridge between her parents. Her knees are virtually locked, and she holds her hand to her mouth—as if to protect herself or hide—perhaps suggesting that she experiences the picture-taking as an intrusion on her. She could easily make contact with some of her siblings, but she is preoccupied with the camera and engrossed in the photo session. She seems very much her father's girl.

The younger son sits on his mother's lap but takes his cues from his father. He fixes on his father's mouth, which further reinforces my feeling that the father is giving directions. Of all the children, the younger son is the most energetic, a squirmer, but he is being held by the mother, who has both hands on him, and the father, who holds him with his right hand, to keep him still. He has little interest in the photo session and is ready to leave the scene, to jump down at any minute. At his age, his attention span is fleeting.

The younger daughter, clutching what seems to be a toy mouse, sits willfully in her father's lap. She has a devilish, mischievous look on her face, as if she is an Eloise full of bottled energy ready to move. She seems scared of nothing. The contrast between the two daughters' faces is rather startling. The younger appears to be far more temperamental and volatile.

Why is the older son on the floor? Is it by choice, or because there is no place for him in the already crowded parental area? I suspect he's where he wants to be since, although he is momentarily fascinated by the photographer or something the photographer is doing, he is basically independent, and is absorbed by his top, with his hand positioned to thrust down the handle and set it spinning.

Even though he's content, there is something disturbing about the older son's face. Look closely at his mouth and eyes; they reflect a glazed, blank, or sick look. When I first saw the photo, I knew something was wrong, but couldn't come up with any explanation that satisfied me. Bothered by the obvious problem, I showed the photo to a doctor who is an eye, ear, nose, and throat specialist. Within seconds, he made his one-word diagnosis: adenoids. A subsequent interview with the parents proved him correct, and further demonstrated how much our prior training affects what we see. I can't remember seeing more than a handful of people with an adenoids problem in my life, and while I knew something was wrong, I couldn't identify it. The physician, who may see several cases a week, made an immediate identification.

Now that we have been over the photograph once, we should go back and scan it to see what we've missed so far. Start from the upper left corner and read the photo from left to right and downward as you would a book. Take your time; look for unusual details.

As I reach the middle of the photo, I notice something strapped to the older daughter's arm. Obviously a child's pocketbook, you say. Although in this case it is not an especially important detail, look again. Particularly note the cylindrical protrusion on the side of the object. Doesn't it now look more like a child's camera than a pocketbook? And in the context, doesn't it make more sense? The older daughter was going to be photographed, and she brought her own tiny camera to join in the fun. I point this out to emphasize the fact that with photoanalysis we must not jump to the most obvious conclusion. We must observe in depth, with heightened perceptions, adding up the evidence to slowly reach a conclusion.

As I continue scanning, I see the younger daughter's mouse again. And on the last scanning along the bottom of the photo, I notice the spinning top for the second time. But now I see something I'd missed before, an object between the older daughter's feet. It looks like a harmonica. Four children—four toys brought to occupy them if they got restless during the session. Since the two daughters and the older son have theirs, the harmonica on the floor may explain why the younger son is so active. He has dropped it, and is trying to get down to get it.

The fact that each child has a toy for amusement reflects thoughtful preparation on the parents' part.

Now look at the photo one last time. Is there anything you have still missed? Do you see anything new? Have your perceptions changed, or do you still feel the same?

I hope you have immediately realized that I am trying to trick you, that this is not the same photograph. If you haven't, then I have made my point.

Let's take this second photo, from the same session, and see what has changed—see if we are able to gather any new or different perceptions.

The major effort at containment has now shifted from the younger son to the older daughter. You can see that she is struggling to free herself, but now four parental hands are holding her back, the father restraining her shoulders and the mother holding her right arm. The older daughter is definitely not just a shy, quiet, obedient child.

The younger sister now has a more intense, almost fierce look about her. She is frowning, possibly indicating that she is angry and tired of having her picture taken.

The younger brother has changed his position and is even more active in his attempt to escape and find his harmonica.

The older brother's adenoids problem is even more pronounced than it was in the previous photo. Congestion and pain are evident on his face.

The mother has opened her eyes, and they are alive and warm, further confirming our assessment of her very human qualities. Look now at her hands. They are strong, the hands of a mother who is no stranger to washing, sewing, and cleaning.

The father continues to lead the family, but focuses now on his younger son, and whatever he is saying is probably concerned with keeping him in the group. The second photo reconfirms that the father is the more verbal of the two parents, while the mother is fully able to express her feelings toward the family through touch. It is important to note again that the parents had the opportunity to make physical contact with each other, but

44

again their hands miss. And again the children do not touch each other—not at all unusual for their early age, since they are far more absorbed in their own behavior in front of the camera than in making contact with other siblings.

The space that exists between the father and mother—a distance to which I've alluded before—does give us something to think about. What does it tell us about the future of this family? How close is the relationship between these two? How close will it be ten years after this picture was taken?

In the second photo, facial expressions and body positions have changed, but not that dramatically, and we still feel the vitality, warmth, and exuberance of this energetic family.

As with most of the personal family photographs in this book, after formulating my observations and opinions, I was able to conduct an interview with the subjects to document my findings.

The photos of this family were indeed taken during an exceptionally joyful, happy time. The family was close emotionally, intellectually, and physically, and the children were central to the parents' lives and interests.

The father had many talents and wide-ranging pursuits. He was an engineer, but science, music, and literature were his favorite subjects. He extended himself in many directions at one time, and occasionally he overextended himself. Although at times self-absorbed, he completely adored his children and delighted in doing things with them. He was very physically oriented and loved to take walks, during which he gave the children vital lessons about life and nature. His special way of telling stories and creating moods would enrapture anyone. He had a great love for ritual, and the children felt he was magical. Frequently after dinner he would have the lights turned out and light a candle. Even lighting the candle would be done in his special way. First he would light a match, then a rolled piece of paper, and finally the candle from the paper. Then each child would tell something he or she knew about animals, astronomy, or nature.

Curious about everything around him, the father passed his curiosity on to the children. Life was a high for him, and he was able to completely turn himself on without drugs or alcohol.

While the father tended to be a dreamer, the mother was more practical and down to earth. With four young children to care for, she was swamped with work. She was rooted in tradition and family loyalty, believing always in the sustenance and preservation of her family. She was emotional and intelligent, believed in spiritual things and in psychic connections.

The older daughter was quite feminine, sometimes shy, but always individualistic and artistic. As the oldest child she always provided the strongest bridge between her parents, as she is doing in the photos. To protect herself in times of emotional stress, it was her custom to close herself up, also evidenced in the photos by her locked legs.

The younger daughter was adventurous and frightened of nothing. A fighter from birth, she could be extremely willful and determined. She was headstrong, with a quick temper, and became very much a tomboy. At the time of the photo session, she was much closer to her father than to any other family member.

The older brother was bright, sensitive, and introverted, a loner and nonconformist. He could spend hours alone, playing by himself, and seldom wanted or needed to be with other people. He could burst into wild eruptions if frustrated.

The younger brother was the extrovert, gregarious and on the move. He could easily become impatient and restless, and confinement always bothered him.

The photographer was a close friend of the family. He was an amateur who just loved taking pictures. He enjoyed the family and joined them often, in this instance through the photographs. To some extent, the photos reflect his own desire to have a family like the one photographed.

The personal family interview confirmed our earlier assessment of these personalities in all significant aspects. And hopefully the extended exercise has provided a sense of the discipline and tools you will need as we further explore the potential of photoanalysis.

A further way of looking at the photo can open other doors. Let's imagine for a moment what might happen if the photo were to come alive. What if the individuals started moving? Where would each one go? If you could join them, where would you place yourself, and how old would you be? Your present age? Younger? Perhaps older? How would you feel as you approached the group? How would you react?

What if the people started to speak with you? Imagine their mouths moving, their thoughts. What are they saying to each other? And what do you say to them? Make up a story about the photo and the events leading up to it. Projecting yourself into photos provides an additional way of gaining insight into your own personality and unconscious feelings.

4.

Rediscovering the family album

Neither words nor the most detailed painting can recall the past so accurately, so realistically, and so completely as a good photograph. This is especially true of your own family photos because you were so vital and unique a part of those photographic experiences.

The photos I'll be using in these next chapters are all from personal family collections. They were selected to demonstrate the range and depth of psychological insight that becomes available through subjecting personal photos to photoanalysis, and to represent the types and varying qualities of those found in most private collections. With the exception of a few studio portraits, they were not taken by professional photographers, were not intended for publication, and are, therefore, sometimes not of the best quality. None has been altered or touched up in any way except, in a few cases, to improve their reproducibility. In most instances, they are reproduced in their original size.

The space of one book makes it impossible for me to analyze *all* the significant meanings in every photo. I have therefore limited my comments to each photo's most important points; this allowed me to use more photos and provide greater variety. Where appropriate, have included validating information from the interviews conducted with the people who allowed me to use their photographs for this book.

This photo is the first in a series of portraits of the same family as it developed over the years. The picture is almost one hundred years old, and was taken soon after Daguerre introduced nitric acid and a copper plate to a camera obscura, making it possible to reproduce "in light and shade" the image photographed. At the time, photography required a lengthy, tiring sitting without movement because the exposure time was painfully slow.

Our first impression here is of a youngster posing informally for a formal studio portrait. The unusual position of crossed legs and hand-supported head suggests a practical solution to the problems of a lengthy sitting for the young child. The head and body convey a relaxed, comfortable sense of self, and the facial expression transcends posing, offering a reflective, knowing, almost wistful look. The child's face seems somewhat older, more mature than the body.

The most startling thing about this photo is the child's sexual ambiguity. Without background information, we cannot tell just from the photo whether this is a boy in a dress or a girl with a boy's haircut. It was not unusual a century ago for young boys to wear dresses and long, curly locks, but it was unusual for girls to have their hair cut so short. Girls normally wore their hair long, either flowing or braided. This, therefore, hardly seems a picture of a young Victorian girl, but it is. But why did her mother give her such a boyish look? Had she wanted a son instead of a daughter? Did the mother fear later sexual rivalry?

From my interview I learned that this young girl considered herself "dominated and squashed" by her successful, vivacious mother.

Zürcher Engros-Lager Julius Brann
ZÜRICH, Bahnhofstr. 75.

The girl in the preceding photo has now married and
become the mother of three children. Notice that she has
not done to her older daughter what was done to her.
This child has long hair and is the model of feminine
attractiveness. The generation-to-generation cycle is
broken.

The portrait photographer obviously asked the family to
look in a specific direction holding their pose—slightly to
the left of his camera. But even his "hold still"
admonitions cannot stifle the individual reactions. The
son stands proudly by his mother's side with a bemused,
almost impish smile, while the older daughter holds her
flower basket, her stoic expression suggesting
resignation. The mother now has long hair, braided and
in a bun, and is holding her younger daughter, who gives
the impression of being a wild little gypsy.

But where is the father in this family?

Julius Brann   ZÜRICH

This photo was taken by the same photographer in the same studio as the family grew. The little "gypsy" girl has now become a beautiful doll-like child. Her older sister holds her hand protectively to insure she doesn't fall. The son continues to substitute for his missing father, standing close behind his mother as an indication of his role as surrogate head of the family. He has drawn himself up to full height and assumes an air of masculine pride and capability.

As the children have become older and more independent, their individual personalities continue to emerge and become more defined. They have moved from their mother's all-sustaining cradling to take positions as active members of the family. In their place is the newest addition, so the mother still has her "doll" for company and pleasure.

But why is the father still missing? His absence is becoming more noticeable as we go along.

The family, now full size, consists of a son and five daughters. And the father is present; he exists. All the other family members are locked in a typical portrait pose, looking slightly to the left of the photographer, but the father displays a will of hs own and centers his complete attention on his youngest daughter.

She is obviously the favorite, and has the place of honor between her parents in the center of the family. She gets physical contact from both parents. Her mother holds her right hand, and her father has his right arm around her back and his left hand lightly touching her knee.

The father is so attentive to the youngest daughter that he literally has his back to an older daughter. She is stiffly formal and appears quite unhappy in her exclusion from the family nucleus.

All the daughters have their hair up, but in strikingly different styles, with the older daughters more daring and innovative, an indication of old-fashioned parents' gradual relaxation of control as their children reach maturity.

In my validation interview, I learned that the youngest daughter was and continued to be the parental favorite. She was spoiled, pampered, and treated like a "little bird in the nest." The father's absence in the previous two photos is explained by the fact that he was hospitalized on several occasions for tuberculosis. In fact, the two earlier photos were taken specifically to be sent to him in the hospital.

Strange happenings. Some of the subjects' eyes are open, others shut, and some faces reflect discomfort. And why the strange dress, the costumes? This is no ordinary family portrait.

The occasion was a silver wedding celebration for the parents. The photographer used phosphorus to brighten the room, but the extreme light became blinding for some. The two oldest daughters, standing behind their parents, have just completed a play in their honor, thus the costumes.

The parents sit close together with arms linked, the mother with her silver anniversary wreath in her hair and her arm linked around her husband's.

Now the mother, holding her first granddaughter, is obviously enjoying her efforts to cheer the distressed child. This is the first photo in the series in which the mother has broken into an open, free, spontaneous smile, and her entire face radiates with joy.

What strikes me most about this photo is the drama evident between this mother and her mother (the old woman with the white shawl). The old woman is the same mother who, in the first photo of this series, allowed her daughter's hair to be cut so short as to make her appear boyish. She has maintained her own elaborate hair style, even in old age.

The contrast of facial expressions is also revealing. The little girl's great-grandmother looks on grimly, in disapproval or even contempt. Her hands are tightly clasped, and her upper body leans away from the little girl. She alone fails to share the pleasure of the rest of the group.

What messages are her narrowed eyes sending out? Is it anger because the child is causing a scene? Or is she angry because she wanted to hold the child? Does she feel she could have done a better job of the photo session? She and her daughter obviously have a completely different approach to the problem. One would like to cheer the young girl into joy; the other would melt her into submission and good behavior with a stern look.

57

The family has again increased in size. The son, leaning on his father's chair, has before him his wife and new child. The oldest daughter, directly behind her mother, is with her fiancé. The parents have the seats of honor—central, comfortable, surrounded by their children—and both are thoroughly enjoying this occasion. This family photo is obviously less posed and more relaxed than the preceding ones. There is a mixture here of warmth and seriousness; the individuals are more free to express what they feel.

What intrigues me most about this photo is the relationship between the two sisters standing between the two men. The younger sister, on our left, stares straight ahead with sealed lips, ignoring the older sister, who looks at her intently, her lips slightly parted as if she were speaking or about to speak. Her eyes fix on those of the younger sister, but there is no return look, no acknowledgment.

The indication of attempted communication without feedback is evident not only in the faces. The older sister is trying to make contact through touch, extending her right hand and arm around her sister's shoulder. With her left arm, she reaches toward her younger sister's right arm. You can see (behind the father's head) that some contact has been achieved. Their hands meet and most likely touch. But again the younger sister controls the contact, even limits it with her left hand, which she uses as a barrier by clamping it down on her right arm. The more glamorous older sister—with fashionable hair style and long earrings—is persistent. She wants the contact, and unconsciously she wants her attempt at com-munication recorded by the photograph.

During an interview with the older sister, I asked her to have a look at her participation and communication with her younger sister in the photo. She was startled. "What am I doing there?" she asked herself.

How typical, I thought, to collect such photos and never really look at them. This is what most of us do.

She continued, discussing their relationship. "I wanted

her to accept me, to understand me, but she never did. I
felt so estranged from my family; no one accepted me. I
was always the 'bad' child, and she was the 'good' child.
I dreamed of devils and she of angels. She was the
moralist, religious. She even married a preacher. We
were totally different—opposites. I would exaggerate,
and she would always call me a liar. I ran away from
home to study acting, and at that time that was as bad as
being a prostitute. When this picture was taken, I had
just returned home from my studies for a visit. I felt more
confident, and I wanted a different relationship with my
good sister. I remember how disgraceful everyone
thought it was for me to wear the earrings, but I wore
them defiantly. I was trying to resolve, to change my
relationship with my sister, but it never happened."

This series of family photos has not only captured the
physical developmental changes that have occurred in
individuals, but has also recorded some of the dynamic
psychological forces at play within the family. The series
records tensions as well as joys and dramatically
illustrates not only the existing interpersonal
problems—for example, between the two sisters—but
also shows the older sister's attempt at resolving their
problem.

To my dear aunt
Henrietta

5.

WHAT HAPPENED
WHEN WE WERE YOUNG...

Even though he is sitting very still and upright in the first
photo here, this baby seems relaxed and content. From
the photo on the left, we cannot be sure he is a boy, but
the combination of hair style and dress in the second
gives stronger indications. (I later confirmed it was a boy
through my interview with the family.)

This photo is rather dramatic for a studio shot. On
first glance, we are drawn to how the boy touches his
crotch with both hands—as if holding or playing with his
penis—and to his slightly mischievous look. As we notice
how uninhibited, how free he is, we wonder why a parent
or the photographer didn't object, why someone didn't try
to prevent him from touching himself. If they had, he
either wouldn't be touching himself, or else his facial
expression and body posture would have been different.

When we look more carefully, however, we realize that
the boy is not playing with himself at all. Instead, he is
holding a ball of some sort. We can see the curve of it as
he clutches it and protectively holds it to his crotch area.

This photo emphasizes the necessity of making sure of
our perceptions and not jumping to conclusions. We
must make sure we see what is there, not what we want
to see.

Now the boy is being held by his glamorous, outgoing, attractive mother, but his attention is not with her at all. It is still with his ball, which we can see clearly now. As in the first photo, he indicates a sense of possessiveness as he clutches the ball to himself for balance as well as contact. His mood and his attachment to the ball are consistent with his attitudes in the first photo.

Most youngsters have a favorite stuffed animal or doll or blanket for security. This baby has his stuffed, soft fuzzy ball to fulfill his security needs, and in this photo he is more trusting of the ball than of his mother.

This adorable little girl stands attentively in her chair. She seems happy and excited, but has a shy, surprised air about her. There are conflicting feelings here. If you cover her body with your hand and look only at her face, you see her open-eyed, faintly smiling look. Yet when you cover her head and look only at her body, you experience her tension, her slight nervousness, her shyness, her raised shoulders, and her fidgeting with her dress. The dress looks so clean and pretty that she may be consciously or unconsciously holding it as a protective measure to keep it from getting soiled.

As with many people, the different parts of the girl's body tell different stories and express different feelings. In my interview with the girl—now an adult—she remembered the occasion as her birthday party. Her dress was new, made especially for the party, and she had explicit instructions from her mother to be careful and keep it clean.

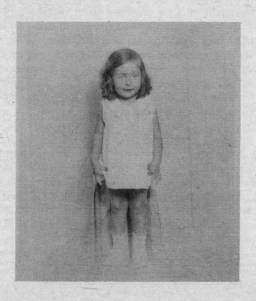

This photo is of a typical pre-World War II Swiss public school class. The benches are formally and geometrically aligned, as are the students.

Let your eyes wander from face to face along the rows of students. What feelings are evoked in you? Would you like to join this class? I wouldn't. There is a dominant repressive and defensive atmosphere in the classroom and precious little joy. Most of the faces are either defiant, unhappy, blank, scowling, or pained. Of the thirty students, only six smile or reflect any warmth. Is this atmosphere the result of a reaction to the photographer, or is it a reflection of the students' attitudes toward the teacher, who stands grimly in the back and to the side?

Do you notice anything special about this class in addition to its attitude of discontent? Look at how the students are packed in like sardines in the last rows, while in the first three rows they are spaced out and less crowded. Also notice the difference in age and physical size between the two groups.

Because I am personally familiar with the facts behind this photograph, I know that, except for the two children on the extreme left, the remaining ten children in the first three rows are all repeaters—they have been left back one or more grades. And following the old, idiotic dictum that children will pay more attention if they are seated in the front rows, these students were placed up front—at the foot (and mouth) of the teacher. No doubt some of the defensiveness and general unhappiness comes from those students' sense of humiliation and embarrassment, especially at having their pictures taken. To them, a photographic record is being made of their failure.

The room is also depressing. About the only signs of life are two plants on the teacher's desk. There are so many symbols and possible emotional expressions that are life- rather than death-affirming, and yet—as you can see—so little life-affirmation is present in this room where these children spent the major part of their days.

Here's a photo of a school costume party. The children seem generally happy, but if we look closely we see a considerable range in feeling from joy to depression. Some bodies are stiff, others relaxed. The youngster in the gypsy costume in the front row (third from left) looks particularly unhappy.

If you look carefully into the faces, you will notice that some of the children are boys dressed in girls' costumes. Their hair, which could positively identify them as boys, is covered with hats and scarves.

Since I am the boy in the gypsy's costume, I am pretty damn sure of my perceptions here, that the unhappiness is caused by the boys being dressed as girls, at their teacher's instructions.

This is a group of Sunday school girls with their teacher. Look carefully at each student. Which two girls would you pick as being sisters? What clues would you use as evidence?

Parents frequently dress siblings alike, even when they aren't twins, and here the two girls with the same tilt of the hats, and the same coat with white collars, are sisters. Now that you know, you can also tell that their facial features are similar.

The hats worn by most of the men in this photo as well
as their ages suggest some kind of fraternity. And the
formal clothes, party decorations, and setting in what
seems to be a ballroom indicate a dance. Most of the
subjects here are in a formal and dignified pose for the
occasion, but there is also some spontaneous play that is
quite out of place. Examine the faces and hands and see
if you can find the playful drama.

The lady in white sitting in the center of the first row
has given her full attention to the man on her left,
undistracted by the man at her feet—who is lovingly
caressing her ankle and, seemingly, kissing her knee.
The other young man sitting on the floor looks on in
obvious amusement and, perhaps, envy.

The unusual feature of this photo is the young man's
ability to break free from the formality demanded by the
situation. The photo was taken in the 1920s in a
Swiss-German city where on such occasions complete
formality was the rule, usually ironclad. For the young
man to break the rule took considerable spontaneity,
risk, and a playful sense of self.

Contrast the attitudes of the two fathers in the following photos.

In the first photograph, the father proudly holds his baby on his knee, keeping the child at arm's length because he is visually oriented and is more interested in viewing than in close physical touch. He has set the child on a pedestal—his knee—and admires her as if she is the most precious thing on earth. His delight lies in what he sees and holds, and he is far more interested in communication with the child than with the photographer. We get the impression that his participation would be exactly the same even if the photographer were not present.

This father will not be intimidated by his crying baby. He is going to pose for the photograph come hell or high water, and his smile transcends the baby's tears and screams.

The baby wants no part of the scene, and appears to have been dumped into the father's lap immediately prior to the photo being taken. The father is posing and posing the baby. He makes no effort to comfort the baby, but balances him for the photo. His communication is strictly with the photographer, and his child, at least as far as this photo is concerned, is only an object.

In this photo, both mother and baby are equally focused on the photographer—most likely the father. They are lying on a bed, relaxed and thoroughly enjoying the event. The mother protectively touches her child with her left hand and her touch is returned. The baby, who could easily have dropped his right hand, reaches up and grabs his mother's ring finger.

Their facial expressions are neither blank nor posed; they reflect joy on the mother's part, rapt attention on the baby's part.

It is not true that mothers and fathers unconditionally love their babies. The presence or absence of love depends on the communication they establish and the feelings they develop. This mother and baby are off to a good start.

This mother radiates a sense of loving care and a certain pride as she looks down on her baby. Her smile is neither excessive nor understated. She conveys warm support to the baby, who looks somewhat startled and slightly apprehensive—probably at the newness of being photographed.

In this photo a young mother lifts her baby, with real joy
on her face. His expression of displeasure could be
because he fears heights, but if so, it is doubtful that this
loving mother would do anything to activate or intensify
his fear. More likely, the baby has been crying, and
swinging him through the air was the mother's effort to
cheer him up. He still looks teary-eyed and unsettled
even though his mother firmly supports him with her
hands, arms, and shoulders.

What to me is unusual here but very positive is this
mother's playfulness and spontaneity. Usually it is the
father who involves himself in such physical playful
activities.

Here are two nude children totally absorbed by their play in the sand while a mother sleeps and suns herself. The youngsters are filling a wooden truck with pieces of driftwood. They are so preoccupied with their labor that they remain almost unaware of each other, and neither notices that their picture is being taken. This is a good example of spontaneous, collaborative effort. But see how dramatically the whole scene changes in the following photo.

Their communication has obviously changed radically. What do you see happening in this photo? The boy has become aware of the photographer, and the girl has become aware of the boy; but let's see exactly how.

She has a startled, defensive reaction as she visually focuses on the boy's penis. She looks fascinated, entranced, curious; she might even want to touch him out of curiosity if she were closer. Well, if that's what you see, then you're dead wrong.

If you look closely at the boy, you will notice that he has just turned toward the photographer. His feet are still turned in the direction of the girl. His left hand is open, to the rear, and slightly raised. His spread fingers suggest that he has just released the falling stick in the background, which the photo has caught as a blur. The girl is looking toward him, sure, but at the stick rather than at his penis, and her hands are raised, not to touch, but to protect herself from injury.

This photo should emphasize that appearances can be deceptive. All too often we tend to see only what we want to see or what we think we are expected to see. But that just won't work if photoanalysis is to be meaningful and successful. Instead, we must look carefully at all the elements in photos, and add up the evidence, making sure that in our study of central elements we do not overlook background details.

Anyone who wonders how early we develop the physical ability to express a wide range of different emotional feelings need only look at these five baby photos, which reflect joy, hurt-pouting, curiosity, contentment, and a conventional photographer's pose.

But what happened to this boy's freedom in the later photos? In the one above he sits defensively in his chair, his right shoulder raised, his jaw set. We can almost experience his discomfort, his body tension. He's squirming around, about to climb the walls. Can you imagine the physical energy required to keep such a defensive body stance, to be so on guard? This photo was taken by his sister, and they battled occasionally.

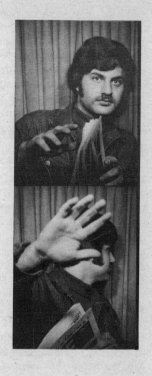

Now look at the sequence of four-for-a-quarter photos (a photography-class assignment). In the first, the boy is hidden behind his newspaper. In the second, he has lowered the paper just enough so that he can make eye contact with the camera. In the third, he guards himself with raised hands, and has his right shoulder defensively elevated. Finally, in the fourth, he turns away from the confrontation, again using his hand as a shield. In the series we have a reaffirmation of the theme of the single photo.

The young man in the photos was raised in an authoritarian home, his father being a naval warrant officer who frequently admonished the son with phrases like "Let's square things away," and "Let's get things shipshape." The son, unwilling to submit, always had difficulties in coping with authority. His move is to do the opposite of what he is told, and his approach to life is to be defensive and on guard—as his later photos reflect. He anticipates pain, battles, and conflict rather than closeness or warmth.

We can tell a lot about people from observing their relationships with animals. Often children develop more caring and loving feelings for their pets than they can express for humans. Pets provide touch contact, and they are generally straightforward in their behavior. As an analyst, I am convinced that the relationships that pets offer have helped many people avoid serious emotional difficulties.

In this photo, the girl has her relaxed, yawning puppy in her lap. She supports him tenderly, looking down on him caringly and at the same time supporting him firmly with her hands. Her joined knees offer him a secure foundation; he can't fall from her lap.

Her love, care, and concern for her puppy now is extremely good preparation for later life when she may have children to care for.

This elderly couple looks adoringly at their dachshund as if he were their very own child. In fact, we can easily imagine, from looking at the picture, that if a real grandchild were substituted for the dog, they would have the same caring, loving faces. The couple married late in life and had no children of their own, and the dog provided them with a significant and meaningful family experience. When the dog died many years after the photo was taken, the couple mourned as if he had been a real child, and never quite recovered from the loss.

This young girl has her hands full with her struggling cat, which is desperately trying to escape. Part of the problem is that the cat is being held almost on his back—and no cat feels secure in that position. The girl wants to prevent the escape, but the cat wants no part of the situation. She might have had better results if she had first soothed the cat, talking to it, petting it, and stroking it.

Through her developmental years, this girl never learned to love or become attached to cats or any other pets. Some of her distaste and aversion had roots in such experiences as the one recorded in this photo, where her physical ineptness is the basic source of her inability to relate well with the cat. It is just too bad that no one showed her how to handle animals earlier, which could have changed her entire attitude toward them.

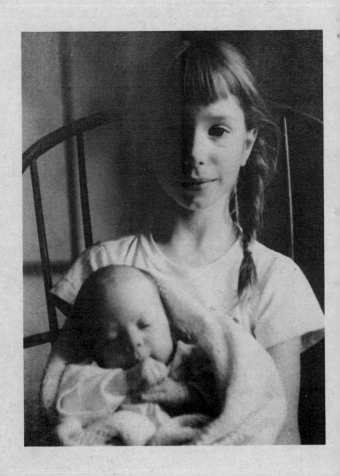

6.

Discovering relationships within the family

The arrival of siblings in a family is always complicated and requires readjustments in family interrelationships. The older child is no longer central or unique, and parental attention will be more spread out. How the older sibling reacts to the arrival of the younger is often reflected in photographs.

Here you see a young girl holding the newest family member. She is neither ecstatic nor depressed. She has accepted the new arrival calmly, and her studied pose indicates that she is trying to be very adult in her care and holding of the baby.

Younger siblings do not always want to be held by older siblings. Here, the older sister is holding her younger brother between her legs as she sits in a lawn chair. Her hold is firm and she looks determined, but her brother is far from settled and content. His arms are struggling, and he is trying to escape by sliding down in front. No doubt he was placed in this spot by his parents so the children could have their picture taken together.

There is no way we can tell from this photo whether this exchange—with the older child determined to dominate and control the younger—will be the major interaction between the two for an extended period, but the photo does reflect that it is a significant aspect of their developing relationship.

With your own photos, you will be able to tell from extended series of photos what types of relationships between siblings developed in your family, and whether and how those relationships maintained consistency or changed.

The "flower girls" on the opposite page are fraternal twins. They look somewhat alike; they are dressed alike, but their personalities are far from alike.

Notice the positioning of their bodies. One twin faces the camera directly, the other sideways. Now look at their arms. The twin who faces the camera directly also extends her arms forward and spread apart, suggesting an outgoing, determined openness. The other twin's arms are enclosed and protective, suggesting that she is more inwardly directed. Now study their faces. One is squinting, almost frowing, and has a strong, forceful look; the other's face indicates softness, warmth, and a gentle nature.

The same themes are evident in the twins' relationships with their flowers. One firmly clasps her picked flowers in her left hand, and even her free hand has formed a fist holding empty air. Her entire presence suggests willfulness, control, and ownership. She will aggressively seek many things and retain what she gets.

Her twin sister almost protectively cradles her flowers in her hands. She has the smaller bunch, but enjoys what she has. We can almost fantasize how each went about picking the flowers: the aggressive, forceful twin focusing on size and number, while her gentler sister picked only those she could enjoy.

The twins are growing up within the same family, receiving similar parental and social inputs, but already we sense very different personalities and lifestyles.

This photo was taken some years ago and accurately reflects the dominant characteristics of the girls as they grew to adulthood. The twin on the left was more dominant, assertive, aggressive, clutching. She wanted more for herself than she needed, and her focus was on collection rather than on experiences, on possessing more than on really enjoying what she possessed. In her relationship with her sister, she hoarded her own things and appropriated whatever she wanted of her sister's. The other sister was more gentle, warmer, more protective.

The more gentle twin married first, but died young. When she died, her sister took over—by marrying the widowed husband! And we can see the aptitude for that in this early photo of the two as children.

One need only look at this photo to dispel forever the
notion that family photos are always posed and are
therefore psychologically insignificant and unrevealing.

Each face here carries its own story. The two girls on
the right are upset, but not just because the sun is in
their eyes. There is tension between them: they are angry
with each other, because they have quarreled and had a
falling out. We can easily see the conflict in the way the
middle girl has deliberately bent her head away from the
girl on the right, indicating that she is the source of the
conflict. Even more revealing is the attitude of the girl on
the left, who is obviously savoring their antagonism. It is
as if she has felt excluded, and can now retaliate by
enjoying their anguish.

Photos can capture various modes of family relating and reflect specific dynamics of a particular theme, in this case teasing or "sister torture." Teasing, as an expression of sibling rivalry, is a common experience for most children in large families. No two siblings interact in exactly the same pattern; each teases in his own unique way, resorts to his own body gestures.

In this photo the sister on the left is sulking; she is moody and distressed, a good victim. Her older sister provokes her by poking and pointing, but she wishes only to be ignored and left alone. This then is to become their pattern for some time.

Before attempting to determine the meaning of the first
photo on the next page, look at both photos and try to
figure out the action taking place between these two
sisters and its context.

Both photos depict an Easter egg hunt. In the first, the
younger sister is about to pounce on a discovered egg.
She looks most determined, and her right hand is raised
and ready to grab. The older sister looks hurt and bitter,
and she is desperately trying to hold back tears by
sealing her mouth. She has probably been saying
something like "This is my egg. I colored it; I
decorated it. It's not fair." But she has been told by
her parents to let her sister find and have the egg.

The two girls are quite different. The younger is
intent on achieving her goal. The older is concerned
with the adult communication with the parent taking the
photograph. In the second photo, the young sister's
goal is achieved, and the prize is immediately placed in
the mouth. The older sister has regained some of her
composure and self-control and accepted the loss of the
egg.

In a later family interview, the younger sister reflected on the photos. "I was a terribly oral person; I used to eat grasshoppers and caterpillars, everything I could get my hands on. I remember once seeing my sister cry and the effect it had on our parents. I decided I would never cry again, and I didn't for many years."

As in the two photos, the younger sister was frequently naked throughout her childhood, and at mealtimes her mother would put her in her highchair naked and tell her to "go to it," whereupon she would indulge in an eating orgy. Such behavior was indicative of her instinctive and straightforward nature, which can be seen in the communication in the photos. On the other hand, the older sister was more intellectual and the parents dealt with her on a different basis.

Early photos like these—especially when they reveal action, as opposed to those that are more posed—can be extremely useful in predicting the most dominant emerging personality characteristics.

Sometimes the detective's approach is necessary if we are to get to the bottom of what is actually taking place in a photo. Here, on first glance we see three girls painting a fence. On further study, however, we realize that only two girls actually have paint brushes. The third girl, who looks slightly sad, is brushless, and yet she is sitting so close to the action that we can't help but wonder what happened to her brush. She seems too close to have just been watching, and her sitting position suggests she was painting. One explanation could be that she was taking turns with another girl, but her forlorn look indicates that perhaps one of the other girls has taken her paint brush away.

That is exactly what happened. The standing girl, a next-door neighbor, simply walked over, took away the brush, and proceeded to paint. In my talk with the victim, she said, "She's always the bully; she does that all the time."

Here are two girls in a sand dune. One poses deliberately through the dune grass with her chin propped up by her hand, while the other is about to . . . what?

Her raised left hand is extended too far for a direct hit with her fist, but her facial expression clearly communicates delicious mischievousness. I don't think she is about to strike physically, but she is definitely enjoying some anticipated prank. Considering the setting they are in—the sand dunes—my best guess is that she has some sand in her fist, and she is about to let it filter down onto her friend.

For years these two girls have been the best of friends—and still are—and the photo, taken some years ago, captures a characteristic aspect of their relatedness: the playful pranks they frequently perform on one another.

7.

Discovering how people communicate

There is an Old World charm in this photo of two sisters at play with their dolls and toy baby carriage. The younger sister pets and strokes her doll's head while the older sister gazes down in enjoyment.

The photo shows complete harmony and cooperation, and indicates dressing alike was an important part of the event. The younger sister is almost swimming in her dress, which is many sizes too large. We can see extra folds of material, and the width is enormous. From this we can guess that the family was very dress-conscious, and that looking and dressing alike were valued. Although the photo is posed and staged, it does indicate the closeness between the two sisters that has continued for over fifty years.

These two sisters are also communicating—in a prime example of imitation imitating imitation. The older sister, on the right, is completely self-absorbed by her make-believe cigarette smoking. She is a study in attempted sophistication as she goes through the motions she has seen at home, in the movies, or in magazines. Her "cigarette" is in her mouth, and she is reaching to remove it as if she has just taken a ladylike puff. Her younger sister holds hers as she intently studies the action for behavioral cues.

In this photo, pay special attention to the encircling arms and hands of the older sister. Through her touch, she divides her attention equally between her two younger sisters, offering to each protection and warmth. The youngest girl, thoroughly delighted, returns the touch, while the middle sister is more self-absorbed and into

herself. She leans her head away and turns her body slightly outward, seeking more separation and independence.

The protective concern for and sense of fair and equal sharing with her younger sisters are central qualities in the older sister's character, and it is no accident that those qualities are expressed in the way the sisters are grouped for the photo.

Looking at your own photos, try to pinpoint those siblings who take on protective attitudes and those who accept the protection. If you have a continuing series, taken at various ages, try to determine how long the protection lasted and what its end signified (most likely the emerging independence of the protected child).

Sometimes we take photos with limited awareness of what we are actually photographing. We see central people, faces and movement, while the less obvious factors often go completely unnoticed. Later, when we look closely, we can be surprised not only by what has been included, but also by the richness of its meaning.

When the father of this family took this photo, he was so intrigued with photographing his wife and new baby that he missed the fact that his two older daughters were literally hiding their faces behind their balloons. But what does their hiding mean? Does their positioning express conscious or, more likely, unconscious resentment at the birth of their younger sister? Do they wish she would disappear, and are they expressing that by disappearing themselves? The fact that they also keep their physical distance and position their arms in defensive positions is further indication of their disapproval.

From my interview with the two older sisters, I learned that their physical distance from the the mother and new arrival did in fact express resentment, and their "hiding" behind the balloons was partially from resentment, but was also inspired by their playful attempts to see through the balloons.

If only the first photo in this series of three were available, we would be hard pressed to explain why the girl in the foreground—the one with the fingers of her two hands touching—has such a pained expression on her face. We can search and search for clues, but more information is needed to discover the roots of her unhappiness.

The second photo makes us aware that something rather dramatic is taking place. The girl has dropped her head and extended her arms outward from her body, as though she were in shock. And now she is the focus of attention of the others surrounding her.

In the third photo we see a pure, uninhibited expression of pain and a cry of outrage. The pain is immediate, intense. The girl's hands are now grasping at her body. What could have caused such a reaction? Did a bee sting her? Is she in pain for some medical reason?

The answer can be discovered by returning to the first photo. The grandmother in the first photo is visually focusing on the girl in the foreground. The grandmother appears to be biting her lower lip and has a look of anticipation, as if something unusual is going on. She also seems to be restraining the baby she is holding with her left hand.

The key to what is happening is in the expression on the baby's face, a firm, determined, almost triumphant look with raised chin. The baby is in the process of doing something physically to the girl in front, like pulling her hair with her right hand, which is out of sight, hidden behind the girl's head.

In the second photo the action has been completed. The camera has caught the precise moment after the pull. In the third photo everyone's reaction is clearly expressed. The girl cries out in righteous indignation, while the grandmother teasingly and playfully confronts the baby she adores for what has taken place. At the same time, she attempts to comfort the hurt girl with a reassuring touch of her left hand, but her primary attention focuses on the baby, reflecting her favoritism and priority. The other girls identify with the pain and intensity of the situation: one simulates a pained expression, displaying empathy; the other picks her nose, an expression of tension.

This series of five photos tells a developmental story
about the relationship between two brothers. In the first
photo, the older brother's beaming smile reflects his
warm feelings toward his younger brother. But the way
the older holds the younger suggests protectiveness
rather than just friendship. Notice how the older brother's
hold has shifted the younger brother's jacket, indicating
that if the older brother released his hold, the younger
would fall. We can discount the possibility that the
younger brother is attempting to break free, since his leg
positions show no movement, no struggle.

The protective hold is repeated in the beach photo.
Again the quality of physical relatedness is protective,
but now the younger brother can obviously stand by
himself.

In the third photo the older brother gathers up his younger brother with his left hand and presses him supportively and caringly against his own body. We have the sense that it is perfectly okay for the younger to lean supportively on the older. The younger is thoroughly enjoying the event and the contact, but it is one-directional contact; it flows from the older to the younger. The older brother is down on his knees, to be more equal with his brother, and to be able to gather him to him.

In the fourth photo, both brothers gaze intently into the camera. There still remains the element of protectiveness, and the effect of all four photos is to suggest that this protectiveness on the part of the older brother is their typical way of relating. The younger brother accepts the protection and takes it for granted. But he seems to be able to manage well for himself, and it could be that the older brother is compensating for something.

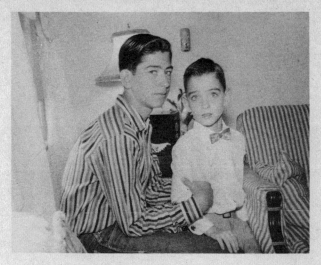

In the final photo, the two brothers, now much older, have come a long way in their relatedness. Now the need for protective physical contact has been broken. They sit side by side, closely, and the warmth is still between them, but there is no longer any need for support; they exist as equals.

(A fascinating sidelight to their positioning in all five pictures is that the younger brother is always on the older brother's left. This could reflect any number of things, but if you will look carefully at the third photo again, you will notice that the older brother is left-handed, as we can tell since he wears his baseball glove on his right hand. In conversations with the older brother, I learned that his left hand is so much more developed than his right that he would never consciously do or hold anything important with his right hand, not trusting it to give him the strength he might need.)

But why the support and protection? The older brother told me that he was eight years old when his brother was born—three months premature. For months after his birth there were severe doubts that he would even survive. As a result of his premature birth, the joints in his legs were stiffer than they should have been and he had much trouble developing proper motor control. Thus his parents and older brother devoted much time helping him to get proper exercise and also became extremely overprotective of him. The fact that he honestly needed so much attention and the wide difference in their ages prevented the older brother from ever developing the normal hostility and resentment usually found in older siblings, and his attitude was always one of care, concern, and protection.

How many different, recognizable emotional expressions are there? Some authorities say less than a dozen, but I feel the range of expression that can be captured in a photo is enormous, if we take into consideration the many subtle variations and combinations of feelings we all can express.

Here, on first glance, we see yet another "nice" picture of a beautiful young girl. Her expression is wistful, dreamy. But is she deep in thought, or is she sad? What is she experiencing?

The slight tilt of her head and the upward gaze of her eyes suggest resistance to the photographer, possibly boredom. Her face and body seem to be saying, subtly, "Oh well, I'll put up with it. Go ahead, take my picture, but let's get it over with."

In fact, the girl was with her family and some of her mother's associates on a country outing. She was the only girl present, and everyone was doting on her. One member of the group—not a relative—pursued her with his camera while she played in a softball game. Mildly exasperated, and in keeping with her character, she finally consented to stop and let him take her picture, only to run off and continue her game immediately after the click of the shutter.

Photos can capture significant feeling we have about friends, because they can activate forgotten memories of past friendships. These three youngsters are obviously happy on this occasion. The girl in the center is particularly pleased, probably because she's in a central position, surrounded by close chums. It would seem she is almost rubbing her hands together in outspoken delight.

In the previous photo, the children were posing for the camera; in the one below they are entranced by their own activities. The feeling from both photos clearly shows their enjoyment of each other. The children are making music together, he strumming his guitar and she beating out rhythms on her drum. This is pure joy for them both, and the photo reflects a close, happy relationship. In fact, the two youngsters lived in the same apartment building. They were good friends and played together often until one family moved away.

Little does this young boy know what is about to happen to him. He's concentrating so deeply on what he's about to pick up from the floor that he's oblivious to the furious little girl. The camera has caught the moment before her direct hit.

Looking at this photo later in life, the girl always saw herself as "holding a book in the air." She completely missed her rage because she never thought of herself as anything but supportive, warm, loving, and friendly, as indeed she is in the following photo. (She's in the John Tallmers Play Group T-shirt.)

This visual blocking of what is actually happening in a photo is quite typical if the person has a stake in seeing himself in certain ways. The desire to negate other, less favorable aspects of one's personality distorts perceptions, and must be closely watched if photoanalysis is to be successful.

The photo above reflects more than just two friendly girls; it would be impossible to get such a shot by posing them. As it is, their faces glow with deep and authentic care for each other. Their looks, their facial expressions, emerge out of real feeling for each other, supported by their arms around each other's shoulders. Interested only in each other, they are completely oblivious of the photographer. The two girls have in fact known each other since kindergarten, and, now almost in their twenties, they have maintained their close friendship.

In the two photos above, a mother and father took turns photographing each other with their son. The photos sharply contrast the differences in physical closeness to the boy. The mother stands erect, like a mannequin at attention. Her extended left arm and hand contact with the boy looks like an afterthought rather than a deeply felt attempt at touch communication. Her dress may well have prevented her from kneeling or lowering herself to her son, but she could have gathered him closer to her. It is significant that the boy's right hand is slightly raised, as if he were unconsciously anticipating some other expression of touch.

In contrast, the father kneels and gathers his son to him, and the son uses his right hand to hold the father's encircling arm. Thus, the son has two very different experiences with both parents. There is no way of knowing whether these photos reflect the typical and sustained sense of physical closeness within the family, or whether the circumstances or events of the day were making the mother feel unhappy and distant from her son. The only way we can finally resolve the issue is by looking at other relevant photos or by conversations with the parents.

117

Here a mother and son walk hand in hand down a
cobblestone city sidewalk. In each free hand they are
carrying things. Their clothing suggests that the photo
was·taken in the 1930s, and they are dressed remarkably
alike. They both wear berets, although slanted in different
directions, and their overcoats have a similar cut and
style.

118

The mother looks pleased and proud to be walking with her son, but the boy is apprehensive and uneasy. His eyes have a concerned, hesitant, distrustful look. Does his look reflect his feelings about his mother or his reaction to what is happening—possibly some strange, unknown street photographer about to take his picture? My feeling is the latter, since the boy is focusing his attention directly on the photographer. If his feelings were toward his mother, they would undoubtedly have been expressed by looks at or words with her, or the removal of his hand from hers. Instead, it seems that he feels an "assault" is taking place. He doesn't lessen his pace, but he seems most unhappy about the photographic intrusion.

This young daughter is pulling the classic disappearing act. She experiences the camera as an intrusion and attempts to cope by hiding behind her hands to break the visual contact. During her younger years this was a typical reaction to being photographed. From my interviews with her, I learned that her behavior was based more on shyness than on playfulness, and to this day she is a person inwardly directed, leading a very private life and avoiding intrusions from the outside world.

8.

How to interpret the many styles of facial and body expression

A single photo can convey many styles of communication. It is obvious in this photo that the father and daughter have a comfortable, loving relationship. Just look at their easy physical closeness. But their loving communication is secondary at this moment, for they are in a teaching/learning relationship. The daughter observes her father intently as he blows across the bottle top to make a musical sound. The father is also reaching for the bottle, either to steady it or to change the liquid level and produce a different pitch. They are experimenting with sound, and that was not the only occasion. Throughout the years their relationship has been one of shared learning, searching, and experimenting, not only with musical sounds, but in all typical life experiences.

In this series a mother (and born teacher) has made reading stories a vibrant, exciting experience. Her daughter reacts with rapt attention; the mother's enthusiasm is contagious. The four photos are extraordinary in that they capture so precisely spontaneous learning communication.

In the first photo the mother acts out sounds and through facial expressions interprets the story while her daughter fixes visually on her face and mouth. In the second photo the daughter shows in exaggerated style what she has learned through imitation as the mother looks on in encouragement. In the third photo the mother switches to a new emotion and again the daughter watches, ready to take in and imitate. In the fourth photo the daughter explodes into her own interpretation.

The mother and daughter are not at all inhibited, for their exchange is genuinely felt. One has the feeling that the person taking the photos must be an intimate, probably an imaginative father, since there is no visual awareness of him from either mother or daughter. He is recording a precious exchange between two very "turned on" individuals, and there is no indication that they are being directed. If only all learning experiences and parent/child relationships were as free and open as in this sequence!

Look at this series of four developmental photos of the same girl and see if you can discover a unifying theme about her physical presence in all the photos.

People have various ways in which they consciously and unconsciously indicate and express their affection in photos, and I think of this girl as a "head tilter." She uses her head by pointing, tilting, or slanting it toward the person for whom she feels affection, or she uses it to snuggle up against the person she feels emotionally close to.

In the first photo she bends her head and leans her body toward her aunt while her mother sits, somewhat separate, to the right. When we talked later about the photo, she said that during this period she was closer to her aunt than to her mother.

You should recall the photo from Chapter 1. In it, she tilts her head toward her father, but her brother's fist makes it impossible for her to get closer. But she is able to extend her right arm around her father's waist—we can barely see her finger encircling him—another indication of her affection.

In the third photo, she is now older, and alone with her brother. What a contrast! She is making every effort to be close, but he is not at all interested. She has her smile and determined body stance, but he has his "I have to put up with this" look. Again her head tilts toward her brother to make the contact. Her face and body, especially her folded arms, suggest her firmness and determination to be close, but in contrast her brother's locked hands indicate his self-containment and his attempt to seal himself off from her.

In the last photo, we have a happy threesome. The girl became a young lady, and again she is between her aunt and mother. But now she tilts her head toward her mother, and also takes her arm. The emotional closeness has shifted from aunt to mother (which she confirmed in a conversation), but the aunt is not upset, and she joins in by making contact with her niece herself.

When looking at developmental photos in a series, we should always be alert to consistent or unifying themes, such as the way this girl holds her body and her head to indicate affection. Once themes are found, then you can get down to the really hard work of defining the meanings they convey.

On the opposite page are formal school photos of three brothers. They are posed, but even so the positioning of their hands and their facial expressions are remarkably different and revealing.

The oldest son looks self-absorbed, contained, and controlled. His face shows a faint trace of feeling, but he is not about to share it. His neatly folded hands separate and seal off the world.

The middle son radiates warmth, openness, and friendliness. His face and hands are relaxed, and he gives the impression of being a gregarious boy who makes friends easily.

The youngest son has an impish, challenging expression on his face. His hands are open, as if in challenge, and if he were instructed to fold them, he would probably not comply.

After I wrote these descriptions, I talked with the father of the three boys, who told me: "The oldest son is extremely intelligent, perceptive, and lonely, like I was. He's asthmatic; he has difficulty relating; he doesn't get along; he comes on like a wise guy. His insights and perceptions frighten me.

"The middle son is lovable, a bunny. He is perfectly coordinated physically, and much more relaxed than his older brother. He is natural, and gets along well with anyone he meets.

"The youngest son is a little devil. He must have his own way, no matter how he is punished later. Punishment means nothing to him. He's very stubborn."

When trying to unravel the emotional experiences of someone in a photograph, start your analysis by coming up with one descriptive word that captures verbally the whole feeling behind the photo. The photos on the opposite page are of three girls from different families. Each of their facial expressions activates different feelings. Look at the photos and find the words that, for you, best capture the feelings evoked by each.

My word for the first is "diseased," because the "growth" on the girl's lips makes her look like she is afflicted, suffering from some dread skin disease. (Actually, I'm dead wrong here, unless you consider a severe case of "mayonnaise mouth" to be a disease.)

I would say "shock" for the second photo, because the formation of the girl's mouth indicates that the visual impact of whatever she saw was sudden, extreme, and unexpected.

"Disdain" seems appropriate for the third photo, because although one would expect this youngster to be enjoying her ice cream, she obviously is not. Instead, she appears to be toying with it, almost trying to avoid it. The reality of the situation was that she had ordered a flavor—mocha—that was totally unknown to her, but seemed exotic and inviting. When it came, she hated it, but felt obligated to eat it anyway.

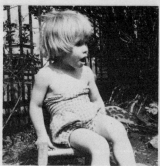

Here's a family outing with sailboat mast and rigging
lines in the background. The young daughter sits
between her parents, yet slightly behind them and
physically apart. They make no attempt to reach her
physically, nor she them. She is happy and self-
sufficient; her hold on the wooden pins for balance
indicates that she is well able to take care of herself.

   What has happened to that cheerful, resourceful little girl? In the second photo she still has her cheerful face, but now, at age nine, she looks more like a mother than a friend of the younger companion she has her left arm around. Note the change in her appearance—the tremendous gain in weight—but also note that she is not self-conscious about it, and makes no attempt to hide her weight.

   Fully dressed in hat and coat, the girl appears to be an elderly woman. Her joy and energy have disappeared, and all that is left is a posed, "plastic" smile. She is actually only eleven years old in this third photo. When I discussed all the photos with her, she looked at this one and exclaimed, "My God, I have no neck."

   The fourth is her favorite photo of herself, taken in Florence, Italy. What a person chooses to stand next to in a photo can be very revealing symbolically, and when the photo is a favorite, we can be certain that it is central to certain self-conceptions. The symbols we surround ourselves with are always significant.

In this one the girl stands next to a statue that looks like a pregnant male riding a turtle over a fountain that is in the shape of a wash basin or toilet bowl. Water gushes forth from the turtle's mouth. Does she identify with the turtle? Is she the turtle, the pregnant male, or the toilet bowl? Her smile seems to be one of resolution, as if she has conquered some deeply significant conflicts within herself. She doesn't need to touch the statue, only to stand next to it in triumph. How much of her choice was conscious and how much unconscious? What has she resolved?

Well, obviously, the weight problem is gone. She has her neck back, and is slim again. But that isn't all that's here. Sometimes it is useful to free-associate about photos, to let your mind randomly touch on any number of possibilities. For example: The statue is androgynous, male and female at the same time. At the time of the photo is she clear as to whether she is to be male or female? Is she realizing the turtle's pace of progress, and change at a turtle's pace is not what she desires? What about early unresolved developmental problems—about birth fantasies, about how babies develop, or her own toilet training and feeding? Is she saying she will need a man to make a baby with, and not be self-contained any longer? Does she want to be able to make a baby without the man, or does she want a man and this is now resolved?

All those themes are hunches, possibilities, and there are more; but we are only speculating. If we were working with the girl analytically, we could ask questions until we had concrete answers. I would start with "You look so pleased with yourself; what have you resolved in this photo?"

In talking with the young woman, I found that she very much wanted the photo to be taken by the statue, and asked a stranger to take it, since she was in Europe alone. She felt the statue was grotesque—like she had been grotesque when she was fat. But now she had changed and was feeling very good about herself. She was using the photo as a comparison, for future reference.

When she was a child, her idea of childbirth was that it happened by giving someone an enema. Later, she did hope that she could have children alone, without any help, like she did everything else—without any help. She always felt the need for self-sufficiency. The other theme she touched on in our conversation was that when she was fat she could run only as fast as the turtle in the photo.

The last photo brings her full circle. She is once again in the middle of her parents and slightly behind them. Something has happened to make happiness return—she is slim again—and it is clear that she feels only good about herself. No one could take away her look of joy, self-sufficiency, and ability to do things well.

Eyes have a unique way of revealing inner states of
feeling, almost as if they connected directly with the
"heart" of man. If we covered this man's eyes, we could
say he is happy, relaxed, informal, and we could observe
that he is drinking something. But only when we look
directly into his eyes and see their glazed, unable-
to-focus look, can we tell that he is drunk, and
that his drunkenness expresses itself in pleasant feelings
rather than in anger, sullenness, or withdrawal.

If we block out the girl's eyes, there is no way of telling her inner feelings, or what she is thinking to herself about the cast on her left leg. Her eyes—betraying bemusement and tolerance of her condition—tell us of her healthy acceptance of painful reality, and show her resources in being able to cope. Even though she has just undergone corrective surgery to stop bone growth in her leg, which was overcompensating for an accidental break some time before, she can still lift her drink in a whimsical toast to her difficulty.

The women below have different attitudes about being photographed. One makes direct eye contact; the other looks down, her eyes suggesting withdrawal and depression, and she certainly is not interested in having her photo taken. The contrast in their dress is also startling. The woman on the left is bedecked with furs and has her lap dog and extravagant hat, while the woman on the right sits covered with a plain shawl, looking as if she is straight from a peasant village. She is being given mail, but looks totally disinterested and far away.

The photo was taken on visiting day at a state hospital; it clearly and dramatically states the situation.

Here's an old Coney Island portrait photographer's studio with its convertible-car prop. Subjects climbed in and had their pictures taken.

In this photo, the younger boy is beaming expansively in the company of the older girl, who is too old to be his date yet too young to be his mother. He appears almost like her mascot, and in fact she did take him along on her dates with other men. She condoned his cursing and youthful outbursts, and liked him as if he were her younger brother. He, in turn, had his sexual fantasies about her as he experienced her and watched her on dates. She was his aunt—his mother's younger sister.

This photo reflects an important and common developmental experience—the relationship with an older person who serves as a model and guide to future life experiences that the younger person will be undergoing—in this case sexual.

140

These two photos show the pride and admiration this daughter has for her father. They are allies, and she wishes to model herself in his image.

In the first photo they are both in uniform—he in his Swedish home guard clothes, she in her new school uniform. She is delighted with herself and the occasion. Her entire body—the way she stands, the way she positions her left arm, the set of her mouth—radiates her pride.

141

In the beach scene, which is unusual in our culture, but not in Sweden, she not only admires her father but also seems to be imitating his physical stance.

The same physical distance in both photos suggests an absence of physical relatedness, and the rigidity of the father's stance suggests that emotional relatedness might have been difficult for him. In both photos, the direction of admiration clearly flows more from daughter to father rather than from father to daughter, and there is no mutual exchange.

In my interview with the daughter, she told me that the first photo was taken on her first day of school. She was quite proud of her father, and pleased not to be a little girl anymore. Her mother took the photo, and since the mother didn't have a uniform, the daughter felt even closer to her father. Whenever the mother criticized either daughter or father, the other would rally to the defense; the mother referred to them as "two peas in a pod." The daughter deliberately patterned herself after her father, although she always wished he would relate more to her physically.

142

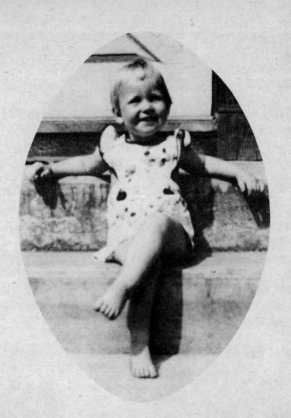

This little girl learned early to show her legs when photos were taken. All three photos, taken at different developmental stages before puberty, show how she has learned to draw attention to herself through her playful leggy showmanship.

First she sits on steps, happy, relaxed, with her arms propped up and open. We wonder what prompted her to

144

cross her legs, since she would have been much more natural with both feet on the ground, but already she is showing herself, her self-importance, and her legs. At this early age she seems to have already caught on that looks are important.

In the next photo she not only shows her crossed legs, but she also forms a church steeple with her fingers, confirming the message that she feels central and important, that she is the star of the photo experience.

In the lower photo she has added a more playful, sexy look while sitting in the grass. She poses, almost provocatively, again bringing attention to herself through her legs.

In all three photos, the girl is imitating adult female role models, yet she is still young. I am told by the girl, now an adult, that no one suggested or encouraged the poses; they were her own choices. Clearly, however, something in her experience suggested them and continued to confirm for her that they could elicit a desirable response.

Through photos like these, and the one of the two girls playing at smoking (page 100), we can easily see how adult inputs influence the development of children. In some cases these inputs are healthy and should continue; their adoption indicates proper maturative progress. In those cases where the imitation is not desirable, photoanalysis offers a perfect opportunity for taking proper corrective measures.

This is what I would call a magical photo, straight out of
a fairy tale. Wearing her crown of leaves, the young girl
is surrounded by growing plants, and she holds more
leaves in her hands. Her mood is reflective,
introspective, the personification of innocence. She
appears to be separate from, and yet paradoxically
together with, the natural camouflage that surrounds her.
She has become, in this photo, a very real part of the
growing life that encircles her.

   After seeing this photo, if we airbrushed her out and
left only the plants, it would seem quite sterile and
barren even though the plant life would still be there. For
she is part of and represents the total mood of virgin
innocence.

In looking at this photo we sense that the two girls on the beach are good friends. Indeed, their faces reflect genuine happy feelings, but in this case looking at their faces tells us little about their similarities or differences in personal feelings about themselves. Here, bodies tell the tale.

The girl on the left has her legs together, side by side, while the girl on the right has her legs apart. The same is true of their arms. The girl on the left has her arms by her sides, while the girl on the right has her arms open in a circular form, resting on her knees.

This kind of body positioning is usually unconscious, and I believe if we had a series taken of them that their positioning would remain consistent with this photo and with their personalities. It would be extraordinary if their positions changed drastically, because the ones shown here are so reflective of their basic personality characteristics.

The girl on the left is more closed and introverted, while the girl on the right is more extroverted. Whether that will continue to be true throughout their lives we cannot tell, but it certainly was true at the time the photograph was taken.

The girls were always close friends, but opposites, and their personalities reflected how they were raised by their parents. The girl on the left was expected to behave, to be a proper, nice girl. The girl on the right was encouraged to be bold, outspoken, and rebellious.

Here's a young body in motion, performing cartwheels on a beach. We are unable to determine her emotional feelings, but we can see a girl with an exceptional sense of oneness with her body. She is a superb example of control and freedom blending together in body movement. Some people feel awkward living in their bodies, but this young girl is completely at home in hers. Photos of moving bodies can quickly and accurately differentiate between those people who are awkward or at ease with their bodies.

Here's a picnic on a rocky island. The grandfather is in the middle with four females to the right and four to the left. What impresses me most about this photo is the couplings—the pair groupings. Everyone is in pairs except for the youngest, yet no one was directed to come together for this photo, and the particular pairings that are captured occurred unconsciously.

The favorite daughter is with her father, and she is beaming. The mother is with the oldest daughter. The two recorder players are off by themselves. The youngest children are near their mother. Each person is with the other person who was the most significant to him at the time, and the overall feeling is one of a happy occasion for all.

Each of us varies in the number of people we are comfortable with at any given time. Some of us prefer to be alone; others feel more comfortable with only one, two, or three other people, and yet others are happiest in large groups. Look at your own photos and see what you can tell about the groupings in them.

Here's a lovely photo of two young people in love. Recently married, they seem to have made a good beginning. They do not need to have their arms encircling each other; we experience the loving vibrations between them without their physically touching. This is the kind of photo that anyone would like to have of his own parents, communicating that they are happy together and yet also separately very much themselves.

The same feeling is communicated in this boating scene. The couple stops briefly to pose for the photographer, their faces reflecting their inner happiness and contentment.

In the series of three photographs on the next page, a wedding has just taken place. What do you feel is the non-verbal message between the newly married couple? What aspects of their relatedness do you think are most significant or revealing?

Their facial expressions and body positioning are certainly meaningful, but what I focus on is their hand communication. In the first photo, the bride reaches out with her right hand and presses it between her husband's closed left arm and body, while he seals his hands together. In the second photo, her hand is still at his arm, but slightly lower, while his hands remain clasped together. In the third photo, her hand has now dropped completely to his hands as she reaches to make contact with her fingers. He returns the touch slightly and also inclines his glance more in her direction, yet still maintains his locked-hands position.

The bride has clearly reached out for the contact and perseveres, but the groom is self-contained and defensively seals himself off from her advances. He does, in the final photo, offer a return gesture, but it is only a gesture, not an adequate response.

This couple did separate many years later, and, while I would never claim that these photos predict that, they do point to the obvious and early difference in their receptivity of each other.

This photo is of a father and son. The son is genuinely pleased with himself and with the photo. He is more informal and relaxed than his father, with his right hand in his pocket and his coat unbuttoned. He exudes an air of success and confidence as he holds his cigarette jauntily in his left hand.

The father is formal with his overcoat buttoned and his left hand held stiffly behind his back. The space between the two men is significant. One holds his hand behind his back, and the other sticks his in his pocket to make sure that they don't touch. Yet there is no explicit antagonism there. It is clear that they admire each other, so long as the distance is kept.

The son from the previous photo has become a father and sits with his grown son. They are deep in serious conversation, unaware that a photo is being taken. The son is speaking and the father is listening, but not particularly liking what he is hearing. The father has a grim, serious, disapproving expression. The two are neither in verbal agreement nor personal harmony. The distance separating them is the distance they need for conversation—a distance strikingly similar to that in the photo of a generation earlier—yet they encounter each other directly with no evasion.

As we examine this photo, we realize the close physical relationship between this grandmother and her granddaughter that has existed throughout years without change. In this photo, they both have intense, almost fierce, yet playful expressions on their faces. The granddaughter is delighted with her place of honor in her grandmother's lap.

In the photo below, there is the same close physical relatedness, which reflects the feelings they have for each other. They both have a similar smile, and again the grandmother has her arms around the granddaughter as the girl stoops and leans against her grandmother. Would that all family relationships could be sustained so well for so long!

Above are two sets of parents with their children. The younger girls stand in front of their parents and the older girl in front of hers. We can see that it's a happy occasion, but is there anyone's face that startles you? Do you notice anything strange?

Right; the father on the left has his tongue sticking out, but the question is why. If it were an expression against the photo session, I doubt that the rest of his body, and particularly his relaxed hand on his daughter's shoulder, would indicate such participation.

Actually, it is quite simple; he was wetting his lips before the photo—as he always instructed his children to do—but the shutter caught him in the act. Such instructions were typical of his participation with his children generally.

This is an example of photographs that cannot be completely analyzed without background information to provide facts about the meaning of specific behavior.

This man's face has changed dramatically since the photo on the previous page, where he stands on the right with his family. Here he looks as if he has not slept in weeks. His darkened face reflects agony and pain. The dark area around his eyes and the general form of his face all point toward suffering, either some emotional or physical calamity.

Two weeks after this photo was taken, the man was hospitalized, and later died of a brain tumor. At the time of the photo he was enduring what he thought were endless migraine headaches with no relief, and he spent every night walking trying to relieve the pain. He was a very brave man who was attempting to hold onto life just as he clasped and interlocked his fingers in support and control of himself.

Compare the two photos on this page. What feelings do you have?

The first is of a man on the move. He is saying yes to life, taking his hat off to the world in open greeting. He is forthright and there is firmness and determination in his face. He sets a vital, lively, steady pace. He is not ambling along. He is well-dressed, but not formal; his suit jacket and coat are open. He greets us not so much with his face as with his hat, and that gesture reflects gaiety, humor, and spontaneity.

The second photo presents a study in contrast. The first is life-oriented, the second is death-oriented. Now the same man is all buttoned up, with a sense of resignation, depression, heaviness, and closure. His hands are tightly intertwined and closed. All the earlier energy and vitality are missing. The man is now in inner turmoil. His eyes are dark, and there is a frown of pain on his upturned lips.

The photos were taken approximately five years apart. Several weeks after the second photo was taken, the man committed suicide. That photo does not predict that he would kill himself, but it does show the shocking physical change that took place over the years.

In the first photo in this series of three, the younger sister appears to be in a "helping" communication with her older sister. She stands resting her hands on her sister's shoulders, and looks as if she has just completed helping her with her hair and shawl—trying to make the sister appear attractive. In the second photo, taken shortly after the first, they stand together, but the attention has not made the older sister feel happier or more attractive.

In the beach photo the same "helping" theme appears again. The younger sister attends to her older sister's hair, trying to make her feel attractive—with similar negative results. The fact is that all the attentiveness in the world will not change the older sister's self-esteem as it relates to her excessive weight. Only loss of weight will make the difference for her.

Here are two radically different faces of the same young woman. The first is a classic, aristocratic pose in which she looks beautiful, elegant, proud. The second photo has captured a burst of spontaneous playfulness. She has just turned toward the camera, breaking free of the need to pose formally.

How many adults can still allow such freedom of expression, or even muster the necessary feeling to let it happen? She sits, windblown, at the bow of a boat. Glass in hand, she is toasting: "Aren't I terrific" or "Look at me," and she has an easy, free communication with the photographer in which the humorous play must have been appreciated.

In her own words, she says, "I didn't feel so good that day, with my stringy hair and dress, and I didn't want to be just another person on the boat. I wanted to be different, and what I did just came to me."

164

166

9.

ONE PHOTO MAY NOT SAY IT ALL

The following nineteen photos were selected from a family collection of several hundred stored in a shoe box. The ones I have chosen to use, a representative sample of the entire collection, reflect the significant developmental stages of a growing son.

Examine all the photos (but *do not* read my observations until afterward). Then make up a story about this boy's growth, using the photos as a stimulus to your imagination. Center first on the more obvious, factual themes that you notice, and then let your fantasies run free in order to enrich your story. After you have completed your story, read my analysis and then the son's brief personal story.

Here's my story.

The young girl sitting on the car fender with her girl friend is not afraid to show her legs. She raises her skirt flirtatiously, as she enjoys her own sensuality and playfulness.

She becomes a mother, almost too soon. She looks more like the baby's older sister, but she shows no

regrets and thoroughly enjoys her child. The little boy,
dressed in his snowsuit, is certainly off to a good start in
life because we feel the family warmth, joy, and unity in
the first family photo.

In the two photos of the mother with the boy, this most
attractive mother has a youthful charm and joy about her,
and she is not afraid to communicate her vitality and
sense of life to her son. The father, on the other hand,
encourages his son to be a "real man" by learning how
to box and to take care of himself.

The beach photo above reflects a genuine playfulness between mother and son, and the photo taken on the roof suggests that some of the physical, sensual relatedness between mother and son can be sexually provocative. He is touching himself, and it is significant that he feels free enough to be able to do this in front of the camera.

In the next group of family photos there is a dramatic change in appearance, especially in dress. As a family, they have become extremely clothes-conscious. The son, who appears to be about seven years old, is still an only child, and is dressed in adult hat and fancy suit, an obvious attempt at making him appear like a "little man." The mother is overdressed and excessively made up. Judging from her son's age, she is in her early twenties, but her clothing and face make her look as if she were in her early forties. What happened to her youthful, playful look at the beach only a few years before?

The next photo of her reveals even a more dramatic change. In her black dress and long gloves, she appears sexy and very provocative. The photo seems not even to belong in the series, and we have the feeling that something dramatic has happened within the family. Since the father appears in no more pictures, the assumption is that the parents have separated.

The separation—as indeed is the case—and his mother's new appearance and attitudes are complicated for the son to cope with, and he is sent off to military school.

Now the son stands proudly and happily with his mother, and we have the feeling that she is proud of her "little man" in military school. I can't help but notice the surrounding symbols in this photo—for example, the cannon pointing in the direction of the arch in the stone building—and standing near such symbols is undoubtedly an unconscious choice in this case.

Next the son is home for a visit, and he's in his mother's bedroom. It's as if they are both preparing to step out for an evening date together and are prepping in the bedroom mirror. The room reflects the mother's femininity and her connection with childhood joys through the beautiful doll on her bed.

In her next visit to her son at military school, we see that the mother's elaborate dress and accessories could very well be a source of embarrassment to him.

The last photo of them together comes as a complete surprise, and is almost a throwback to former days. He is not in uniform, and neither is she! She appears young again; she is attractive without the costume or elaborate hats. This is a happy occasion, but not lasting.

In the last two photos the mother has returned to her preoccupation with elaborate dress and make-up. This makes her appear hard, and she looks as if she is in her fifties, when in fact she has only turned forty, as evidenced by the date on the photo.

The entire series, viewed as a whole, seems to show two completely opposing sides to the mother, each one battling for expression. There is her warm, youthful, wholesome, motherly side, and her exaggerated, showy, erotic side. The photos indicate that neither side ever wins, but they continue to alternate.

Now here is the son's brief personal story:

"My mother married very young, when she was fifteen, and I was born when she was sixteen. I was meant to be her little man, to earn a million dollars and take care of her.

"My parents were happily married at first, but things gradually changed, and when I was eight they separated. They actually divorced about twenty years later when my father wanted to remarry. My mother cast off my father because she feared he would set a bad example for me, being in and out of work and gambling everyday. She thought I'd end up as a gambler or a truck driver. They fought constantly.

"When he left I became her whole world, and she was very ambitious for me. To support us, she first worked in a bakery, but then switched to bars because there was much more money. She kept crazy hours and her looks changed. She changed from being pretty to looking like a prostitute; she had a harder, overdressed, sexual look. Later I was sent off to military school.

"I matured early, and I remember being very jealous of the men in her life. She became more flamboyant and grotesque. Men gave her things, and she made many of those elaborate costumes herself, costumes which embarrassed me on many occasions.

"At my wedding she was very angry and upset. She made faces at my wife and me and kept saying, 'You ungrateful kid; you little bastard.' Many years went by before the bitterness between us changed. Now we can talk and relate, but on a different basis, which allows me to get in touch with my loving feelings for her—feelings which have been repressed for years. She has her life and I have mine. She's no longer trying to hold onto me in any way."

10.

How to find out what public photos actually reveal

I have always been fascinated but perplexed that most books, magazines, and newspapers include many photographs, but they are virtually "thrown away" with few textual references. Whatever is said about them usually consists of something like "From left to right are . . ." Okay, we have identified them. But what then? Usually nothing of real interest or significance. But isn't there something more on those photographs? Something we may not learn just from reading the text about the people or the situation involved? I think there's a lot.

While the previous chapters centered on photos from personal family collections, this chapter will use material from public and professional sources. As you undoubtedly noticed, the previous chapters largely contained photos of children and children with parents, which is typical of the content of most family photo collections. Family photos are taken to record the growth and changes within families, and those photos tend generally to be taken more frequently in the earlier life of a family than in later years when the children are grown, living their own lives and developing their own families.

This chapter will deal largely with adults, some famous, some not very well known, and others obscure except for some brief moment in their lives when they were thrust into the public eye—and before the lens of a photographer.

As in the previous chapters, I will not attempt to write all that I see in each photo. Such efforts would drastically limit the range and number of photos I could present. Again I will focus on what is particularly striking or significant, always bearing in mind what I feel will be useful in helping you to become more visually alert and to see not only what there is to see in a particular photo, but also to generalize and transfer your awareness to other photos.

In the preceding chapters, I had the advantage of being able to interview those individuals pictured in each photo. In this chapter, I have had no such advantage. There were no personal interviews, and no opportunities to validate my observations. I pretend to be an authority on no one in this chapter. In going through thousands of photos for this book, I chose only those that I thought interesting and made some kind of significant point. What you have here is my own educated guesswork. It may not be the whole truth, and sometimes we will never know. What reading I did about the people in the photos was purposefully little—enough so that I could get facts and dates correct, but not so much that my reading might have contaminated or altered the psychological significance I found in the photographs.

Find the Führer in this photograph. One of the children in this school picture is Alois Schicklgruber, or Adolf Hitler, as he later became. It's a typical fourth-grade class, like the kind any of us might have been in if we had attended an all-boys school. The difference is that one of these boys as an adult tried to dominate the world.

Study the faces, the body postures, the positioning. Imagine for a moment that you are Hitler as a fourth-grader, and you already have some mind-blowing plans. Where would you place yourself as this class photo was about to be taken? Holding the fourth-grade sign? Close to the teacher?

Hitler is in fact in the exact center of the top row, not only central, but also slightly higher than anyone else in the photo. "Deutschland über Alles" was the German World War II battle cry, and in this early photo it's "Hitler über Alles!" What the photo shows, in all too chilling dimensions, is that Hitler's personality was set at a very early age.

Adolf Hitler verläßt die Festungshaftanstalt Landsberg
am 20. Dezember 1924

Now, twenty-five years later, Hitler has just been released
from the Landsberg fortress. As you look at this photo,
you can easily see that he hasn't changed a bit—he is
still preoccupied with omnipotence and power
aspirations, despite his recent prison sentence. The
manner in which he grasps the car suggests not only
ownership strivings; it also seems that his right hand is
the umbilical cord that will feed him power directly from
the car. His exaggerated sense of presence and power
stance reflect the inner weakness that he so. desperately
needed to cover and hide.

The grandchildren of Joseph Stalin are being interviewed in their Moscow apartment. The official Moscow news release accompanying this photo read, "They are not in the least disturbed by the reported defection to the West by their mother, Svetlana Stalina, Stalin's only daughter, and said that she will only rest in Switzerland for a short time before returning to Moscow."

The discrepancy between those printed words and the sorrowful, despairing faces of this young man and woman is undeniable. Which do you trust—the printed word or the printed photo? Do you see these faces as "not in the least disturbed"? Or is it more likely that someone was writing a false story with total disregard to the telling reality of the photo, and that, lacking the appropriate objectivity, he tended to see just what he wanted to see?

This is a photo of Alexander Solzhenitsyn, Russia's foremost living writer. I have never seen a deeper furrow chiseled into someone's forehead. Here is a man who carries the impact of his experiences on his face, and this face bears testimony: to the pain of the slave-labor camps, the terror of the cancer-ward experiences, the confinement in a special secret prison for scientists, the anguish over divorce, and the continuing attacks on and suppression of his writing by his government.

This face is a good example of the fact that we learn our looks, we are not born with them. We are born with the genetic potential to look a certain way, but our emotional experiences determine how our features develop and the way they set.

In this photo Solzhenitsyn is attending a funeral. His face cries out a message of sorrow, but it is more than momentary sorrow for the deceased. The look conveys the eternal pain of a man who has suffered for a long, long time. We experience the pain especially in his saddened, sorrowful eyes. But notice the powerful, determined jaw and mouth. Pain has not crushed this man or destroyed the clarity of his vision, which is reflected in his imaginative, original, and deeply honest writing.

Despite the living hell he has been through, Solzhenitsyn remains life-oriented; he has not been and will not be broken. Try in front of a mirror to duplicate his furrow on your own forehead, and you will realize the muscular effort and sense the emotional tension this man has repeatedly experienced. But there is a quiet strength that is overwhelming here.

As this young woman speaks into the microphone, what
does her facial expression say about her inner emotions?
Is she making a political speech? Participating in a
debate? Or are the stakes much higher? What does she
anticipate? And what is the difference between her
expression and that of the young man standing beside
her?

Her face shows dread as well as courage and suggests she is pleading for some top-priority issue. In fact, she is Ilona Toth, twenty-five, pleading for her life. She was a top Hungarian medical student found guilty in a Budapest court of killing a secret policeman during the Hungarian uprising in 1956. She injected gasoline into the neck of the undercover agent because he could betray the anti-Soviet underground newspaper *Elunk* (We are alive). In this photo, she is making a plea for clemency before the court. Her plea failed and she was hanged.

The man standing next to her was editor of the paper, and the stakes were different for him. He was sentenced to three years in prison. In the dynamics of their facial expressions we can easily see the difference in their predicaments. In hers are terrible fear and dread; in his, merely resignation.

Now that you know the facts, look at the faces of the spectators and see how they reemphasize the seriousness of the matter. And look at the young woman's hands as they clutch her notes—her plea. Her fingers are extended with strain as she grasps the only hope she has left.

Sometimes when trying to capture the essence of an individual from a photograph I find it useful to make an animal association. It's not that I think the person is an animal, but the association helps in finding fresh symbols and words that will make the photo come alive.

Look at this shot of William F. Buckley, Jr. If you had to substitute an animal for the presence captured in this photo, which would you select? What animal does he remind you of? I'd say he looks like a strutting rooster. definitely King of the Barnyard. To me this animal association has more impact than if I were to say here is an arrogant, pompous, self-absorbed speaker. How lifeless compared to the image of a strutting rooster!

Now look at the photo more closely. As he makes his point, Buckley's entire body rises to the occasion. He exudes dominance, superiority from every pore. His facial expression, complete with wrinkled forehead, his raised shoulders, his right hand with pointed finger, and his supporting left hand on the chair—all convey the same message and reinforce each other.

How would you—or do you—feel at the receiving end of that pointed finger? Does it make you want to listen? Or does it make you angry? Doesn't it give you the sense that he is "up there" and we are "down here"? That he is talking down to us rather than with us? Buckley leaves no room for anyone else's thinking or importance. He is master, not to be challenged. This need to exaggerate his superiority suggests that he is compensating for some weakness, because if he were sure of himself, of his abilities and ideas, he would not need to flaunt his dominance.

Let's follow the previous idea of animal associations.
When I first looked at this photo of Vice President Spiro
Agnew giving his election victory speech, I immediately
thought of a bulldog. His whole body and facial gestalt
suggest this: the deep-set eyes, square jaw, solid build,
firmly planted stance, and look of stubbornness. This
man is no light adversary, as many people have already
found out. That powerful head, neck, shoulders, and
general stance suggest he is up to tangling with others
and that he can be extremely willful, rigid, and
tenacious.

Unconsciously, my bulldog association may have
surfaced not only for visual reasons. In England a
"bulldog" is a university attendant employed to enforce
the rules of behavior for students!

191

In this political confrontation New York's volatile
Congresswoman Bella Abzug makes her point with
raised hand and extended fingers as Governor Nelson
Rockefeller attempts physically to retrieve the
microphone. His participation is forceful; both hands are
on her right hand and arm as he attempts to wrestle the
mike from her. He is not interested in any of the other
available microphones; he wants Bella's back—not only to
express his own ideas, but also to silence hers. She
looks triumphant, while he looks angry. Both speak
simultaneously and vigorously, and their highly charged
encounter is readily evident in their wide-open mouths,
which are almost visually interchangeable.

   This photo is a great relief from the usual posed
political photos; the encounter is intense,
spontaneous—and meaningful, to them and to their
audience.

Political and church leaders have consciously or unconsciously realized the importance of using their hands to communicate or buttress their feelings and ideas. The following three photos are examples of hand power.

In the first, a young minister (facing us on the right) effects the "laying on of hands" in an effort to faith heal. The photo is a study of energy "transfusion," with the central person receiving life or healing energy from the surrounding group. Look at this photo; notice the intensity centered in his face and left fist. He is "willing" a cure, and believes that sheer physical impact will have a profound effect. And while we can be somewhat dubious about the effects of faith healing, we cannot deny that what he is doing must have a powerful emotional effect on everyone concerned and particularly on the person being "cured." His left hand symbolizes and demonstrates his spiritual and energy resources, and his right hand—like the tube in a blood transfusion—conducts the flow into the head of the sufferer.

193

In the next photo, Billy Graham demonstrates the same power of hand communication. Like the minister on the previous page, he uses his left fist for impact and reaches forward with his right hand, but his touch here is symbolic. Yet, through the dynamic use of his hands, he is able to reach an audience verbally with the same impact that the minister did physically.

In the photo of Daniel Berrigan at an anti-war
demonstration, his hands communicate as intensely as
those of the minister or Graham, but here the intent has
shifted. Berrigan is not interested in overwhelming
anyone with his presence. His hands express control,
self-containment, and restraint. While the minister and
Graham are actively and outwardly motivated, Berrigan's
hands indicate inner strength and the kind of passive
power that we associate with Gandhi.

Here are four clergymen in conversation—and non-verbal communication. Even a brief glimpse of this photo tells you how essential their hands are in supporting and amplifying their communication. Cover their heads with your hand or a blank sheet of paper; concentrate a moment just on their hands and fingers. What are they telling you? You discover that the hands are quite sufficient in telling a story by themselves.

There are two separate pairs of dialogues occurring in the photo. In the dialogue on the left we see a right hand raised and cupped to reinforce a message. The recipient of the message extends the fingers of his right hand to table level. They are resting, listening, yet responsive, and perhaps poised to rise again.

In the dialogue on the right we see "steepling"—the forming of a church steeple with the hands, which frequently reflects inner confidence, occasionally even a pontifical smugness. The priest on the left has created a higher steeple than the priest on the right, suggesting that he personally feels more power, more importance, or that his point is more significant.

Hands, like handwriting, can readily differentiate individuals. Each set of hands has its own unique characteristics, just as the hands of a farmer are dramatically different from the hands of a pianist or a college professor.

What can you tell about these hands? What would you guess the person's occupation to be?

The hands are delicate, the fingers aged, relaxed, and interlaced. They are aristocratic hands, and could not possibly be the hands of a blue-collar worker or laborer. The hands were those of Bernard Berenson, the collector, art critic, and acknowledged authority on Italian Renaissance art.

No two people walk exactly alike, and our personal walking styles have psychological significance. The following four photos are shown to demonstrate how people feel about themselves and particularly how the emotions they experience directly affect their walk. Pay particular attention to the contrasting use of hands, the way the people carry their bodies, and the nature of their interaction with the photographer.

We don't even need to see this woman's legs to realize she is walking—her freely swinging left arm and her forward right thigh (under her coat) indicate forward movement. She walks steadily ahead, either oblivious to being photographed or unconcerned about it. She appears totally preoccupied and extremely depressed. The downward tilt of her head suggests a sense of heaviness, of personal tragedy. The woman is Nadia Alleluyeva, Stalin's second wife, walking on a Moscow street in 1932. Several weeks later she committed suicide by shooting herself.

This aristocratic woman walking down a present-day Peking street is an unusual sight. She has refused to substitute her regal coat for the drab, uniform clothing of those in the background and emerges as a breath of fresh air. Wrapped in her indifference, she passes like a stranger through a world she no longer recognizes. Yet

she is resolute, unwavering, and unafraid. She is uncowed by authority, and we get the impression that she wouldn't stand aside even for Mao himself.

The lack of joy in her face does not suggest depression as it did in the face of Stalin's wife, but rather self-containment and the strength of inner resources. She has herself and that seems sufficient, even in a country that has long since overthrown all the values she cherishes.

Joseph Stalin's walking style can be summed up in one word: power. Imagine yourself walking with him. Where would you walk—beside him, behind, or in front? My better judgment tells me that I would walk behind him—and be damned careful not to step on his heels.

There is warmth and a slight look of bemusement as Albert Einstein walks with his cane and papers in hand. He does not need to exaggerate anything—by either strutting or dragging along. There is nothing he has to prove; confidently himself, he radiates a sense of worth and competence. The photo was taken in 1920 outside Einstein's laboratory in Berlin, after he had already become world famous for his theory of relativity, published in 1905.

Just as no two people walk alike, no two people sit alike. How and where you sit reflect your personality, your feelings, and how you experience yourself. In the following four photographs you can see that everyone has his own unique way of sitting, and that each person surrounds himself with strikingly different props.

It would be hard to conceive of these four people as interchangeable. The artist Edward Hopper, for example, would never hold the hand of an Egyptian statue, nor could we seriously visualize Katharine Hepburn sitting in a chair like Charlie Chaplin. I don't mean to imply that the same people always sit the same way. Sitting depends on personality and immediate exper- ience—what is happening to the person at that particular moment—but if you study extended series of a person sitting, or walking or talking or gesturing with his hands, you will find a significant number of characteristics that relate to the person's personality.

Hopper exudes tension and determination. Although his legs are casually crossed, his whole upper body suggests tension, which is especially noticeable in his viselike hand grip on the arm supports of his bench. This photo illustrates how a person—or a photographer—structures the environmental props for a photo. Hopper sits well in the foreground with his studio house in the background along with a distant figure. The stage setting is startlingly similar to many of Hopper's paintings. Like them, it is stark, powerful, and psychologically stimulating because you are immediately drawn into speculating on his meaning.

Jean-Paul Sartre, on the other hand, shows no body tension. He sits casually, relaxed, bemused, whimsical, as he gently and humorously holds the hand of the Egyptian statue. He and the statue form a philosophical couple, and Sartre looks as though he is thoroughly enjoying the occasion.

Chaplin leans back into his chair, personifying pomposity. His generally exaggerated manner characterized by his sense of self-importance is caught in his hand positioning and facial expression. He is swelled with pride, and looks as if he is about to receive some very important visitors. As a matter of fact, the photo was taken in 1969 as he was preparing to announce plans to return to the screen as a comedian. His raised left shoe captures his inner tension as he awaits the arrival of the press.

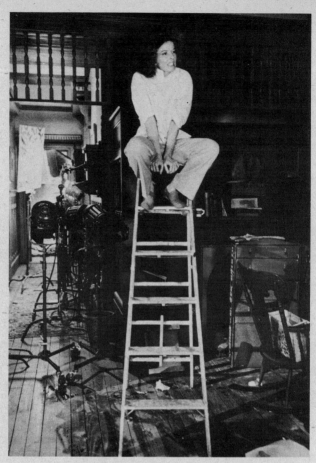

In the photo of Katharine Hepburn, she sits atop a ladder on the film set of *Long Day's Journey into Night*. Her expression is emotionally intense, and everything about her—feet, hands, arms, shoulders, face—is consistent. There is a unified theme in her positioning: She is like a coiled spring about to be released, or a cat about to pounce.

With regard to emotional expression in photographs, many skeptics say that we cannot differentiate between the real and the fake. Look at these two photos and we'll see. Which do you think expresses genuine emotion? Neither, one, or both?

The photo at the top is of Alan Page, the first NFL lineman to win Most Valuable Player honors. He is posing for photographer Max Waldman, who instructed him to snarl and say "AAGGHH!" And while on first glance he looks pretty ferocious, if we really analyze the photo, we see it is a pose. His almost relaxed eyes, his exaggerated open mouth, and his hands with open and spread fingers do not spell out intensity of feeling. There is no congruent body commitment.

The photo above is of a separatist demonstrator
assaulting a Canadian police officer during a scuffle.
There's no doubt that these people are really feeling
what they are doing. Look at the demonstrator's clenched
fists, his gritted teeth, and the fierce expression in his
eyes. They reflect a totality of commitment to his
purpose, and his emotions and actions are genuine,
all right.

Surrealism is an art style that attempts to interpret the workings of the subconscious mind as manifested in dreams. The irrational disparity of the objects in this photo is every bit as bizarre as the paintings of the artist who is the photo's subject. He is Salvador Dali, who has made the shocking his trademark.

Dali is sitting on a wheelbarrow, painting in the Paris Zoo. His tiny canvas is supported by a large easel, and his object of study is an enormous rhinoceros in captivity. In addition, he seems to be using the "Lacemaker" Dutch masterpiece for inspiration. The props are an extension of him, could easily be interpreted like a dream, and make the photo as surrealistic as one of his paintings.

Before reading my reactions to this series of photos, consider them yourself. What is significant to you? How would you link the four photos together as a dream, fantasy, or story? Do you in fact think they form a connecting series?

The first photo is a cluttered introduction to a series, and it is easy to become distracted or preoccupied by the endless themes the various props suggest. Only by analyzing the remaining three photos can we determine which is significant.

The opposite photo suggests the key link in comprehending the series because it makes prominent what was obscure in the first photo. Here is Dali—minus pants—deliberately and playfully exposing himself, but with eyes closed as if in sleep. He has replaced his wheelbarrow with a driftwood chair. But what prop has he carried over from the first photo? Where is the continuity, the connecting link? It is his cane, which he humorously supports between his legs like a giant, erect penis.

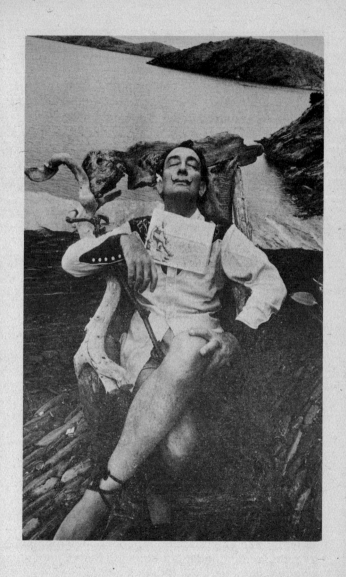

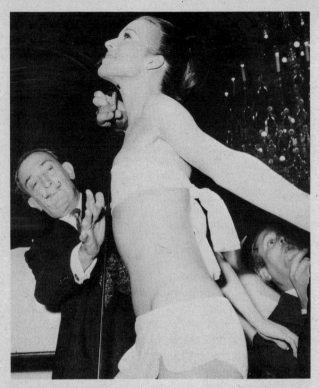

In the photo above, Dali is dressed again as he makes his couturier debut in Paris. His cane is once again central to the photo. Dali has a new idea about bikinis, and he uses his cane to implement his idea. He holds it delicately and directly under the model's chin, with its length extending down the center of her body. He has virtually eliminated the model's breasts. He said he was striving for "the no-bustline look." And he has the model tightly wrapped with a bra to make her breasts disappear. About his bizarre creation, Dali commented in the press release, "All this is to prove that bosoms are too conventional and biological."

In the final photo, Dali appears pleased and animated. His arm is around a Mexican bullfighter, and his cane is shared. The bullfighter has a firm grip.

I think of the four photos like a dream. The unifying symbol is Dali's cane. The cane appears literally to be an extension of Dali, and on different occasions it is inspiring, protective, controlling, magical, playful, sexual, and a friendly companion. It is rooted in power and sexuality, but it also transcends sexuality. He has used the cane to make contact with the bullfighter, and to magically eliminate women's breasts. And what does that say about how he values men and women? He acts through his cane, and in a sense the cane is not only an extension of Dali, it *is* Dali.

Just from looking at this photo, can you anticipate how this sad, almost crying youngster's life will develop? Here he poses with two real guns from his father's collection. He is using them as support, almost as if they are crutches. The pose was most likely his father's idea. The boy grew up in a household filled with weapons and, like his father, developed an unnatural preoccupation with firearms. Up until recent years, most American boys have played with guns, but usually of the toy variety. And we can accurately say that the American people have an obsession with guns, which have played such a vital part in our history. But specifically regarding this photo, it would not be farfetched to conclude that if one day this youngster lost control of some massive repressed rage, he might well use guns as a means of expressing that rage.

The photo is of Charlie Whitman, age two years old. Later in his life he was to climb the Texas Tower and shoot thirty-four people, after first killing his wife and mother. He deeply hated his father.

Even the most astute psychoanalyst could not, from this photo alone, predict that this child would become the Texas Tower killer. But if someone had looked at this photo along with others I have seen of Whitman's early life, and if that person had known ahead of time, as was later revealed, that Whitman beat his wife and that he had once told a university psychiatrist that he was thinking about going up on a tower with a deer rifle to start shooting people, then a mass slaughter might well have been prevented.

I cannot overemphasize how powerful and how important photographic communication can be. The great majority of course show good things about people, but some, like this one, scream warnings that should not go unheeded.

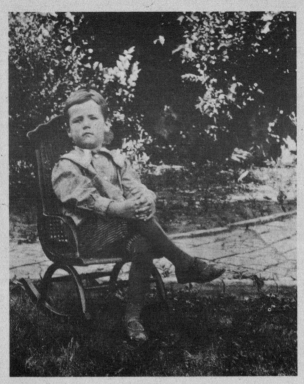

This is a remarkable photo of a prissy youngster in an
exaggerated adult pose. The impressive point here is
that he is not in the least bashful about expressing
through body language his extraordinary sense of pride
and preoccupation with his own importance. The
crossed legs with right foot extended, the clasped hands
over his knee, the haughty jaunt of his head and superior
facial expression all combine to indicate his sense of
self-worth. He is almost saying, "I can do and say
anything I please." You would have to search extensively
to find a similar photo of a youngster.

The man sitting in the chair was once the little boy from
the previous picture. Now there is no need to exaggerate.
He has succeeded in making his mark in business and
on the world. This is Henry Luce, founder of the Time-Life
publishing empire.

Do you notice any relationship between the photo of
Harry Truman as a baby and the photo of him with
Churchill and Stalin before the start of the Potsdam
Conference in 1945?

The baby picture shows Truman playing with his left
foot and reflects tension in his raised shoulders and
around his neck. Compare the baby with the grown man
in the Big Three photo. The stiffness is still there, and is
probably made more noticeable by the casual and
relaxed figures of Churchill and Stalin, who have met
before.

218

Truman's consistent tenseness does tell us that some body language characteristics are imprinted in all of us early in life and become especially noticeable when we are anxious. With Truman, if you will look at a selection of photos of him relaxing with family or friends, you will see a much different man than if you look at a selection of photos of him as head of state carrying out formal duties.

One of the children surrounding the car in this photo will grow up to become President of the United States. Which child is it and who is he?

The child is Lyndon Johnson, and he is in the foreground with his back to the car's engine—its source of power. He is central in the photo, and he is also independent, not content to group himself with the rest of his peers. The sun's glare makes him squint, but he stands alone, leaning against the car almost at attention. (Where someone decides to stand in a photo is more often than not a preconscious choice or a split-second decision, but it is significant and often reflects the values of the person photographed.) LBJ is certainly not there for the ride (on a fender or running board); he is on the ground, ahead of the car and linked to the source of power.

In the next photo, LBJ kisses his father, Sam, good-bye as Lyndon boards the train for Washington, D.C., to take his first job there, on the staff of Congressman Richard M. Kleberg. The startling aspect of the photo is the intimate kiss—certainly an unusual show of affection between father and son in this country. In America we shake hands, possibly hug, but a kiss like this is rare indeed. Before you jump to conclusions about homosexual tendencies, however, read the following passage from *My Brother Lyndon* by Sam Houston Johnson, Lyndon's younger brother:

> When I was about three years old and Lyndon was nine, we used to sleep together in a bedroom off the kitchen next to daddy's room. (Mama stayed with the girls on the other side of the house.) Well, about midnight my daddy would yell, "Sam Houston! Come in here and get me warm."
>
> And I would crawl out of bed and scramble into his room like a little puppy, snuggling my always-warm body against his. Pretty soon he'd fall asleep and start snoring, with me right next to him, holding mighty still and afraid to squirm even a little bit because it might awaken him.
>
> Then I'd hear Lyndon calling me. "Sam Houston, come on back. I'm getting cold."
>
> Back I'd go, moving away from daddy quiet as a burglar and snuggling up to my big brother. But that might not be the end of it. Later on, maybe at three or four in the morning, daddy might get cold again and would call me back to his bed. That's what you get when you've got a warm body; people seem to impose on you.

From that passage we learn that physical contact between males in the Johnson family was common and for Lyndon had early roots. If there was nothing sexual about it, if Lyndon never had any reason to feel inhibited or embarrassed by it, then the physical intimacy expressed in the photo is not at all surprising—it was an accepted part of Johnson family life.

This 1936 Christmas photo of the Johnson brothers (Sam Houston on the left, Lyndon on the right) with their father shows Lyndon's powerful identification with and emulation of his father. Both Lyndon and his father affect the same poses: erect, stiff, with buttoned jackets and hands at their sides. Sam Houston, in contrast, has his jacket open and his hands behind his back. And Lyndon is closer to his father than his brother.

Any number of photos of Lyndon and his father would show the same relationship: warm, intimate, like father, like son. As Sam Houston wrote in his book, about what Lyndon would frequently tell reporters, "I'm merely carrying out the precepts I learned at my daddy's knee."

226

Few people have perfectly symmetrical faces. Imagine you have drawn a vertical line down the middle of a face; there will normally be some slight variation in the two sides, and this difference may increase or be accentuated when the person expresses feelings. Nevertheless, each half of the face should still present the same feelings as the other half. But when one half of a face is in opposition to the other, when it sends out a different emotional message, and when this tends to happen over a long period of time, then there is something highly unusual about the person.

The baby picture on the left is of Richard Nixon at nine months of age. He is apprehensive and sad. And although he is trying to cheer up, to show some responsiveness, he remains frightened and unhappy. His partial wave is tentative and shy, probably a reluctantly ventured gesture to satisfy the admonitions of parents or photographer.

Now look at Nixon as an adult. The photo on the right appeared on the front page of *The New York Times* on August 24, 1972. For the purposes of this discussion, it has been split in half vertically so that you can better see the disparity of its two sides.

The left side of his face (on your right) shows a beginning smirk, the verge of a smile. But the right side is controlled and depressed, full of sadness. Look back at the baby picture. His right side is the one that shows the restraint, and although unsuccessful, it is his left side that attempts some form of social communication through the wave of the left hand.

Having looked at dozens of photos of Richard Nixon, I am struck by the same incongruence of left and right sides. But why? Why are there two separate faces of Richard Nixon, both expressed at the same time? We cannot state categorical conclusions just on the basis of photographs. But we can ask some probing questions.

Is it that his inner emotions are split down the middle, in conflict, with neither side of his personality ever winning out?

Could such disparity be an unsuccessful attempt to block any outward sign of what is going on inside his mind?

Was there never an "old" Nixon and a "new" Nixon, but both existing at the same time?

Nixon has been portrayed as an extremely inwardly directed man, self-reliant and enclosed, distrustful of other people. And for his pre-Watergate closest circle of advisors, he chose the same types of men: Mitchell, Haldeman, Ehrlichman.

I think of Nixon's "peace with honor" slogan when I look at his face. Obviously, everyone is for peace and everyone is for honor. But Nixon felt compelled to exaggerate and emphasize the honor, suggesting to me overcompensation for something dishonorable.

229

Here is a wonderful study in personal contrast and a
most predictive photo—taken months before the
Watergate break-in and the subsequent charges that
John Mitchell was very much involved in the cover-up.
Here, in a unique personal way, each demonstrates how
he will eventually cope with the crises of his or her
public and private lives.

Martha Mitchell looks like a protective tigress—volatile and enraged. She strikes out ferociously at the photographer, whom she sees as someone who is invading their privacy, intruding without permission. You can visualize the flow of words as they explode from her mouth. She is fiercely loyal to John and her uninhibited rage is impressive as she turns on the photographer from behind her sunglasses.

John Mitchell could not be more opposite. He looks straight ahead, completely ignoring the·photographer, his lips sealed around his ever-present pipe. He is contained, stoic, controlled. He is not about to explode like Martha, nor will he try to cope with her.

Think about the photo, and then remember Martha Mitchell's words in later talks with the press. She said, "Somebody is trying to make my husband 'the goat' for the Watergate scandal, and I'm not going to let this happen. . . . I fear for my husband . . . I'm really scared . . . I have a definite reason . . . I can't tell you why . . . but they're not going to pin anything on him. I won't let them, and I don't give a damn who gets hurt." Her words, with their anger and their protective involvement, correspond perfectly with her photographic participation.

In contrast, John Mitchell has remained silent, withdrawn, and unresponsive, as if he is hoping to avoid the entire encounter, as he is in the photo. He does not plan to give anything away.

It's no difficulty to pick out the most important man in this crowd scene. The people around him form concentric circles as they crush in and compete for his attention. The man is, of course, Harlem's legendary Congressman Adam Clayton Powell, Jr., here pictured touring the Watts area of Los Angeles on his way to tell seven thousand University of California students that "black power is the saving grace of the United States."

Surrounded by supporters and over a dozen movie and still cameras and microphones, Powell surges forward and waves—but his wave is not for the people close to him at all, it is for the elevated photographer who took this photo. The people center on Powell, but—master media manipulator that he was—he centers on what will offer him more coverage, a technique and ability that many people in the public or political eye develop an uncannily professional knack for. Make no mistake about it, Powell knew where the action was in terms of promoting himself, as this photo so perfectly shows.

No single group of people is better able to find
photographers and use them to their advantage than are
movie stars, and the late Marilyn Monroe was more adept
than most. In this photo, British newsmen encounter her
upon her arrival at London airport in 1956. Sir Laurence
Olivier (next to Marilyn) and Arthur Miller (behind Olivier
in the white jacket) try to field the bombardment of
questions as Marilyn demonstrates the same sense of
media manipulation that Adam Clayton Powell used in
the previous photo. All the photographers' and reporters'
eyes zeroed in·on her, but she chose not to return their
attention. Instead, her smiling eyes look up to the
cameras that will give her the most impact and exposure
because they can make more of her visible.

What's in a face? Some people's faces look the same from photo to photo. They may reflect either little internal emotion or a kind of photoparalysis in which the person always confronts the camera with the same expression. Other people's faces change depending on inner moods, their relationships with the photographers, and their relationships with others in a photo.

I agree with Ralph Hattersley when he says, "In the eyes alone we can read almost anything about another person." I think of the next sequence of three photos as the three faces of Marilyn Monroe. Look especially into each set of eyes, and you will see that each face reflects a very different inner Marilyn.

On the far left is perhaps the last Marilyn cheesecake photograph, because at that time her fiancé Arthur Miller had chided her for posing for too many such photographs in promoting her film *Bus Stop*. Her face is pretty; it couldn't be any different. But her eyes are vacant and her smile clearly posed—even more clearly "plastic." The smile is used as a mask. She has been told how to pose, and she has complied, but with no inner feelings of pleasure or commitment to the task.

There is something disquieting, incongruous about the photo. Place your hand over her body and look at her face. Then place your hand over her face and examine her body. The total gestalt is not harmonious. There are two distinctly separate parts—a beautiful face, a stunning body. But they just don't go together. The face is saccharine sweet, the expression fake and not in keeping with the sexy, leggy, sensuous body.

The other shot was posed, but now Marilyn's face reflects emotional commitment. It is a seductive, erotic pose. She is proud and haughty with her raised head and eyebrows. Her eyes are sensuous, as is her partially open mouth. If you first cover her face, then her body, as we did with the previous photo, you can tell that they now fit together.

There is commitment in this pose. She stands firmly, legs apart with arms and hands confidently placed. Her right hand is firmly planted on her knee. Her left grips the tail of her costume, ready to playfully put it in motion. The fake cheesecake is gone, and now we have seductive, erotic commitment, even though Marilyn is still reacting professionally to the directions of the photographer.

The next photo was taken immediately after Marilyn's marriage to Arthur Miller in a religious ceremony. It is spontaneous and definitely not posed. Marilyn looks completely different. Gone are the themes of empty, fake emotion. Gone the eroticism. Now she seems completely open and loving, giving her husband a look of pure joy. Her entire face is committed. Eyes and mouth complement each other. Her eyes are wide open, fixed on her husband. They are the eyes of someone apparently deeply in love, and express her sense of deep contentment. The photo captures her genuine look perfectly; no one could look like that without real feeling.

Marilyn Monroe was a professional actress. She knew what was expected of her and she delivered. But she was also human and, like all of us, affected by changes in mood and commitment to what she was doing. The first photo was for publicity, and by that time she could have cared less. She didn't need it; her fiancé didn't want her to do it. The second photo was taken to publicize a charity event in which she was performing. The evidence of the photo tells us that she was willing to give it her all. The third photo is not of Marilyn Monroe, actress, but of Marilyn Miller, wife. Her commitment is not to the photographer at all, but to the joyous event in which she is participating. The photographer captured her in one of those rare moments when she was being herself for herself and for no one else except her husband.

There is something distinctly unnerving about this young girl sitting in a chair, a dog in her lap. It jolts the viewer because in any similar photo of a young girl with her dog, we would expect her to have direct eye contact either with the dog or with the photographer. At the very least we would expect hand contact with the dog. But here the dog isn't even acknowledged. The girl sits listless and indifferent. Her facial expression indicates that she is having no inward experience or that she is in a trance. What could account for such lack of presence? The only visible sign of life is her raised left foot, and it requires energy to hold a foot in that position. Otherwise there are no signs of emotion.

The photo is of Helen Keller at age seven. She is unable to hear or see because at age nineteen months an almost fatal fever left her totally blind and deaf. The photo is even more unsettling when we consider the fact that Miss Keller had no visual or auditory awareness that it was being taken. The photographer could not have communicated with her, nor she with him.

Certainly Miss Keller's blank expression was not the way she looked all the time, and although she seldom smiled at this age, she was capable of the entire range of emotional and facial expressions. These she showed frequently—especially when she was frustrated and erupted in passionate outbursts of temper.

Can you imagine the communications crisis you would experience if you became deaf and blind? Sight and hearing are our primary sensory faculties. All that Helen Keller, and many others like her, had was touch, smell, and taste. Learning for her was quite different than it was for you and I. The next photo demonstrates her unique learning method as she feels the vibrations and movements of Anne Sullivan's lips, who was teaching her. The slight tilt of Miss Keller's head suggests that she is straining to comprehend.

Although she is deaf and blind, there is no question that meaningful communication is occurring between Helen Keller and Alexander Graham Bell. They cannot make visual contact, but it is as if they are having a conversation with their hands. When Miss Keller was six, she met Bell and he was responsible for Anne Sullivan's becoming her teacher. Of that meeting, Miss Keller later wrote, "He held me on his knee while I examined his watch, and he made it strike for me. He understood my signs, and I knew it and loved him at once."

The fourth photo is of Helen Keller's graduation from Radcliffe in 1904. By that time she was already an established author. For her entrance examinations to Radcliffe, she was tested in elementary and advanced Greek and Latin, geometry and algebra. She also learned to speak and write German and French.

In this photo her posture and expression resemble that in the first photo. There is no one to communicate with, only the paper she holds, which is written in Braille. As with her dog earlier, she evidences no significant feelings. If she is reading to herself, as it seems, it is a completely intellectual experience unaccompanied by emotion.

The next photo offers a remarkable study of non-verbal communication. We can tell from the two women's hands that Anne Sullivan is "talking" with Helen Keller through her finger movements. Miss Keller has a slightly bemused smile as she receives the message. This is how the two women looked in the 1920s, after over thirty years of collaboration.

Anne Sullivan was an imaginative, natural teacher. She understood that normal babies learn by imitation, and that babies comprehend what is being said to them long before they utter their first words. She once said, regarding Helen, "I shall talk into her hand as we talk into babies' ears."

The lower photo captures what Anne Sullivan wrote in a letter to a friend, "I spell in her hand everything we do all day long." Charlie Chaplin points forward, and the women all look in the direction in which he is pointing. Anne Sullivan communicates to Helen exactly and fully what is happening. In Helen Keller's early years, she had no idea what the spelling meant, or to what words referred, but now there is complete comprehension. The third woman present is Polly Thompson, who assumed the role of Helen Keller's constant companion after Anne Sullivan's death in 1936.

Compare Helen Keller's facial expression in the photos on the next pages with those in previous photos. There's a striking difference in emotional content. Here she is doing what she did most of her life, and enjoyed most, touching, holding, exploring. She was always insatiably active, almost tireless, since there was so much for her to learn. It would be hard to guess that she

is blind. Her face is alive, responsive, and very much a part of her whole experience as she explores the wheat. Notice how supportive Polly Thompson is. Her touch does not intrude on Helen's experience, but it is there, warm and helping.

Helen Keller's sense of life and vitality is again present in her face as she reaches forward to touch and examine an ancient Egyptian monument. She is not satisfied to simply touch the statue; instead, she must examine its facial expression and features. To do so, she must stand on the bench, and Polly Thompson reaches out to her in a protective gesture, fearing Helen may lose her balance.

The last is an unusual photo in that Helen Keller is posing for a photographer she can't see or hear. Her face is full of emotion, and we couldn't possibly guess that she couldn't see or hear. An inner light shines through her blind eyes. Her wave is an expression of dominance over handicap and a symbol of courage for everyone handicapped, whatever the form.

From this series on Helen Keller, one could assume that the changes in her facial expression and emotional experiencing were made possible through the efforts of her teachers, Anne Sullivan and later Polly Thompson. This would be erroneous. Helen Keller was fully able to react with a complete range of feelings even before Anne Sullivan came to teach. What the series does reflect is that her face became alive when she was subject to direct experiences on a very personal level.

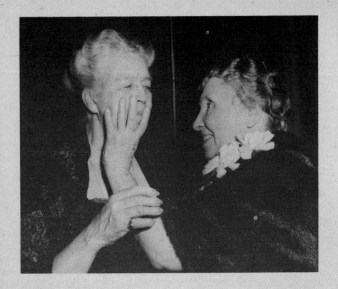

As a child Helen Keller refused to be touched or caressed by anyone except her mother, but that block, out of necessity if nothing else, disappeared gradually. Here is a moving, touching exchange. Helen Keller "reads" the mood in Eleanor Roosevelt's face as we might read with our eyes. The touching is mutual.

Helen Keller's vitality and joy are directly reflected in her face. If we look back over the previous photos, we can see the consistency: whenever she is actively involved in a touching experience, her face reacts. And when she wants to read another person's expression, especially if the person is an intimate friend, her hand goes to the friend's face to "see," as she said, "the twist of the mouth."

This photo was taken as she approached her seventy-fifth birthday, prior to embarking on a five-month trip to the Far East in an effort to inspire and encourage development and expansion of facilities for the handicapped.

Elliot Roosevelt's book, *The Roosevelts of Hyde Park: An Untold Story,* suggests that Lucy Mercer was not the only "other woman" in this father's life and that FDR also had an intimate relationship with his personal secretary, Marguerite "Missy" LeHand. Among other revelations, Roosevelt writes that it was not unusual for him to enter his father's room in the Albany Executive Mansion and find Missy with him in her nightgown.

Can photoanalysis shed any light on that relationship?

In this 1932 photo, President-elect Roosevelt dictates to Missy LeHand in his office as another secretary, Grace Tully, holds a batch of telegrams. The occasion for the photo was the assumption that Miss LeHand would go to Washington as Secretary to the President, thus becoming the first woman ever to hold that position.

The photo, although posed, does capture a warm exchange. FDR is certainly more interested in Missy LeHand than in looking at either the photographer or his other secretary and the telegrams. He gazes with intense care as he dictates, looking directly into her face. She holds her pencil in readiness, but neither looks at her pad nor returns FDR's gaze. She appears shy and self-conscious, restrained and uncomfortable. There is a slight sense of awkwardness in the way she holds her hands. She can't return his gaze for the camera; that would be too intimate. Nor can she look down to her pad; that would appear too formal. Instead she chooses to look "in between."

From this photo, there is no doubt that their relationship was far warmer and closer than the usual executive/secretary relationship. They had mutual respect and care, they really liked each other, and she was devoted, loyal, and admiring. The photo does not support sexual involvement between them. That is not to say there was none, only that there is no direct, tangible evidence in the photo.

The opposite photo is far more revealing. Of the three people in the photo, the *couple* is clearly composed of FDR and Missy LeHand. Eleanor looks like an embarrassed intruder, and a significant space separates her from them. The glare of the sun might have contributed to Eleanor's downward look, and the Roosevelts may well have preferred side seats—thus Missy's position between them—but the cozy way that Missy sits next to FDR is quite suggestive of the relationship that Elliot Roosevelt alludes to in his book.

These photos alone are *proof* of nothing, but they do add visual substantiation to Elliot's revelations.

Amelia Earhart is about to start her fatal 28,000-mile aerial flight around the world. The photo agency caption read, "George Palmer Putnam bids globe-girdling wife goodbye."

Some goodbye! Looking closely at the photo, what do you notice about the couple's relationship? To me, the photo is a perfect example of a husband cashing in on his wife's fame. It makes me wonder who is going to make the flight—Amelia or Putnam? He seems to be taking over, making himself indispensable. And if you follow his right arm to his fingers, you'll see a totally inappropriate gesture. The pointing finger looks like it's making claim to her as if she were his property. The occasion instead called for a more loving, parting touch.

You will recall this photo of the Kennedy family that I used in Chapter 1 to suggest that the boys in the family were central and the girls almost peripheral in their relationships with their parents. In addition we should note the spatial gap between the Kennedy parents. Such physical distance suggests that at the time of the photo Rose and Joe, Sr., related more with the children—particularly their favorites—than with each other. It is possible, however, that because of the number of children, the space was necessary if the parents were to make contact with as many as possible. But since four of the girls are lumped together as a group—and not treated as individuals—I am inclined to stick with my first analysis.

255

Usually, when family members gather for such a portrait, the selection of where individuals are placed occurs preconsciously within each person. There are those who will debate, however, that photo positioning reflects the photographer's directions, and that his directions are an expression of both his conscious and/or unconscious attitudes and values.

Such photographic direction does occur, and usually in more formal portraits, but I doubt that such manipulation was employed in taking this particular photo. The Kennedy family members are self-directed and inwardly strong, and would not passively or tolerantly submit to outside influence. If the photographer was the central influence, then why does John sit so alone, so central, so prominently behind his father? Also, the natural quality of physical intimacy—for examples, Teddy snuggled between his father's legs and Robert with his right arm around his mother—suggests expression more from inner feelings than responses to photographic direction.

In its July 7, 1972, issue, *Life* magazine carried an outspoken, intimate interview with Senator George McGovern. As you read the following quotes from the article, see if you find corroboration for what he is saying from the accompanying family photo. Reading clockwise from 12 o'clock, the photo shows Joseph McGovern, his wife Frances, Larry, George, Mildred and Olive.

"The puritan ethic was a dominant factor in my childhood. 'Make good use of your time' was a phrase I heard a lot."

"Reading and movies are about my only recreation."

"I was painfully shy as a boy. I almost flunked the first grade because I was too embarrassed to say anything in class. Even if the teacher called on me I would refuse to recite. I would not read aloud at all the whole year—though I was an avid reader at home."

"I guess I've always felt, too, that showing emotion is bad taste."

"My mother was a very gentle, soft-spoken person."

"I was always a little in awe of him [McGovern's father, the Rev. Joseph McGovern] though he could joke and kid us too. But there was never an easy conversational relationship. He was so much older—my mother was his second wife, and he was fifty when he married her. He was a very sincere man. I don't think my dad had the slightest streak of hypocrisy in him."

"If there is one thing I cannot tolerate, it is rudeness. I think it is almost a cardinal sin."

Without my spelling it out for you, you should be able to find photographic substantiation for all of McGovern's recollections in the article. Whenever photographs like these are part of an article or book, they provide much more than merely an identification of the people pictured. Photographs are there to be used, to amplify and extend our understanding of their subjects, and not as mere name tags.

Queen Elizabeth poses with members of the royal family
in the Throne Room at Buckingham Palace after her
coronation. In front are her two children, Prince Charles
and Princess Anne, and standing behind is her husband,
the Duke of Edinburgh.

For some, this is a most happy occasion. Examine the
faces. You can easily tell who feels central and involved
and who feels like a prop in an elaborate stage
production. The Queen is radiantly happy; her husband
is warmly present; the Queen Mother wears a bemused,
self-satisfied smile. To the others—the props—sitting for
this photo is more an ordeal than a happy occasion. The
three central "characters" break free from the pervasive
formality to show their human qualities. Yet there is no
doubt that one is looking at royalty with their crowns,
formal gowns, and uniforms.

What interests me is the unwritten but implicit rule that
no one must touch another, no matter how close he might
be standing to someone else. It is just not done in royal
circles. In spite of the crowded conditions, there exists
that distance, that invisible cloak surrounding and
separating each from the other. It is a pleasure to see
the three central faces breaking through royal protocol.

This photo is of Queen Elizabeth and the Duke of Edinburgh with members of the British Royal Family in the official portrait taken on the couple's silver wedding anniversary. What changes have taken place in the twenty years that have passed since the first photo?

First of all, there is more space, and they have made use of the space. The men still stand behind their seated wives, with children scattered on the floor. Now the families are grouped, or at least men and women are paired. There is an atmosphere of informal formality, since this is not a state occasion. But still, as in the previous photo, no one touches anyone else. Each person is again surrounded by the invisible cloak. The absence of touch, rather than resulting from emotional distance within and between families, is a result of social conditioning, long years of royal upbringing. Again the central cast, the stars—because it is their wedding anniversary—are happy and show the greatest warmth. The Earl of Snowden's turtleneck sweater and the Queen Mother's arm extended to her daughter's chair help to break the formality, and now all the faces show more participation and feeling in general. They are no longer just elaborate props in a ceremonial drama.

This classic studio photograph is in direct contrast to most of the candid shots I have used in this book. The photographer is completely in charge, and he tells the family, especially the children, exactly where and how to sit and look. "Fold your hands together, and cross your right leg over in front of the left," we can almost hear him saying. The emphasis is on uniformity, on looking right.

The boy on the right is Martin Luther King, Jr. His parents and grandmother are behind and his brother and sister at his side. These are "good" children, well-behaved and obviously responsive to authority. Yet a photograph that is so totally and obviously "bossed" is hard to decipher; nor are childhood photos always as revealingly predictive as those of Henry Lucy or Harry Truman.

Now, look at this later photo of Martin Luther King, Jr.; it tells a very different story and reflects the changes that took place in his personality through the course of his development. Here he has emerged as an open, spontaneous man. He is comfortable with himself, and his clasped hands reflect a sense of ease rather than obedience. King now has intensity and presence; he is not cowed either by authority or instructions. He is very much himself, in control and "together." Now in 1965 he knows what he is doing.

World leaders—just like ordinary people—have different life styles and personalities. Some are power mad, some are genuinely concerned for the welfare of others, some are deeply suspicious, some are conceptually brilliant, some are cold and reserved, some warm and open. The following photos capture Golda Meir, Prime Minister of Israel and the third woman to become a head of state in modern times, as she encounters her world.

In the first photo, Eleanor Roosevelt and Golda Meir greet each other with mutual respect. Unafraid to touch, their embrace is far more intimate than the usual handshake. You need only glance at the hands of these women to realize that they come from radically different economic and cultural backgrounds. Golda Meir's hands are those of someone who has done strenuous work. In fact, in the early years of her marriage she took in washing to earn extra money; later in her life she worked alongside men in building projects and clearing swamps. In contrast, Eleanor Roosevelt's left hand is gloved, and she carries her right glove, which she took off to shake hands. By no stretch of the imagination could you picture Golda Meir wearing white gloves. It's impossible to associate her with this symbol of gentility and upper-class breeding. Yet the difference in backgrounds doesn't keep the women from genuinely and openly enjoying each other. Arm contact is congruent with their eye contact. It, too, is direct and warm.

In the next one, Golda Meir bids President John F. Kennedy farewell following a meeting with him when she was Israeli Foreign Minister. Their handshake is firm and extended, not the kind that dissolves on touch. And again, as in the previous photo, the physical contact equals their direct eye contact. The photo gives us the sense that these world leaders have touched each other not just physically, but in thought and feeling as well.

Mrs. Meir has always proved herself to be a public figure completely uninhibited in showing her emotions and feelings. In the third photo, she openly grieves at the funeral of her sister immediately following the aftermath of the Israeli deaths at the Olympic Games in Munich in 1972. Her freedom to show the entire range of her emotional experiencing is something we can wish that more of our leaders could handle. But this is something that men in general have been conditioned against. They can show pleasure, anger, but not sorrow. They can't weep.

As Mrs. Meir visits the Milwaukee school she once attended, the hug she gives a present-day student is all-embracing and loving. It is as pleasant for Mrs. Meir as it is for the student. Look at how other politicians deal with children, and you will see exactly how unusual Mrs. Meir is; she gives and receives from *people,* regardless of station in life or age.

Another example of Mrs. Meir's unique qualities as leader of her people is expressed in the next photo as she holds the hand of a weeping Iraqi girl after addressing a rally of relatives of Jews still in Iraq. The rally marked the end of a one-day hunger strike at Jerusalem's Wailing Wall. Mrs. Meir is a *personal* leader, and regardless of matters of state that call for her attention, she feels completely free to offer genuine comfort and support to another person in pain. In a time when most other heads of state feel compelled to isolate themselves for their own safety, this remarkable woman, who is undoubtedly in as much real danger as anyone we can name, extends herself to her people. She is theirs, not vice versa. Her concern and her support are authentic; she is not doing this for photographers. She does not hold back; her impact is through total participation.

In the last photo, Mayor John Lindsay presents Mrs. Meir with the symbolic key to New York City at her official welcoming ceremonies in 1969. Look at how she stands, her legs spread, her feet firmly rooted. Contrast this with how people generally stand, on one foot or the other, with legs close together, concerned for their image. Not Golda Meir; she is firmly rooted to the ground. She is solidly and dramatically present, as usual expressing herself openly and totally.

This series of photos of Golda Meir illustrates the consistency of her earthy, emotional, open, and extremely physical personality. From photo to photo, we always have the same reaction—never afraid to show her feelings, never afraid to express closeness with her body. This is not a fleeting, passing quality; it is central to Golda Meir's existence as a person and as a world leader.

269

Artistic communication, as we all know and as these two
photographs amply demonstrate, is one of the most
individualized means of personal expression.

Above is Pablo Casals, the almost ageless cellist
and composer, a quiet, intellectual, humorous man who
was a consummate master of precision and virtuosity.
Opposite is Janis Joplin, the tragic white blues singer
whose own life echoed the torments of the songs she so
emotionally and so sensually sang.

Criticism cannot diminish their abilities or their appeal in their respective fields. But look at how differently those abilities are expressed. We don't need to hear them to understand the radical differences in their artistry, their styles or their lives. It is perfectly evident to see. Try to imagine Joplin with Casals's cello or Casals singing into Joplin's microphone. You can't do it. They totally reflect their unique personalities as expressed musically and in their lives. Casals is the symbol of control, of a lifetime of persistent study and practice; Joplin was rough-hewn and exploded with raw energy and power; her offstage personality was as dynamic as Casals's is reserved. Yet both musicians could become completely absorbed and immersed in what they created, a process that is superbly reflected in the two photos.

Pablo Picasso—without doubt the most forceful, innovative, creative, and prolific painter of this century. In more than seventy years of creative effort he painted over six thousand paintings, bursting through conventional artistic boundaries. Picasso was a man who could not stop painting. Although quite wealthy, with no need to work, he painted up to his death at age ninety-one, his talent and energy undiminished.

In the above photo, Picasso is elevated on a workbench and totally absorbed in sketching his dove. You feel he is part of his work. Of his approach, Picasso said, "I try to represent what I have found, not what I am seeking. I do not seek—I find." He often painted at night, with light only on the canvas, because he believed "There must be darkness everywhere except on the canvas so that the painter becomes hypnotized by his own work and paints almost as though he were in a trance. . . . he must stay close as possible to his inner world if he wants to transcend the limitations his reason is always trying to impose on him."

We know, then, something about this man as an artist. But how does such a man, such a towering artist, emerge through his personal life? How will he react with his family? Will his vitality and originality emerge in a family photograph, or will he appear like any other typical family man? Let's see.

There were seven significant women in Picasso's life. He started his eleven-year affair with Françoise Gilot in 1944, when he was sixty-two years old. In this photo he is with her and their son, Claude. You do feel that Picasso is the central family figure here, but the photo is generally no different from the usual family photos one finds of stroller being pushed along a beach.

The third is far less typical. The life force emanating from Picasso is impressive but not overwhelming. Claude participates wholeheartedly as Picasso inspires and fires his son with playful, intense emotion. We experience the energy flow from Picasso through his arms and hands to Claude's waist, and Claude responds with raised shoulders and arms and a delicious expression on his face. The life energy is impressive; Picasso can clown, play, mime—he is emotionally and physically involved with his son. We can sense, at least, that Picasso's ease and enjoyment here might not be limited to his son, but would hold true for all children. How many family photos would you have to look through to find such a father-son photo? And how old is Picasso in this photo? He is actually sixty-seven years old, an age when most men are grandfathers. Once, when asked the source of his energy as he neared ninety, he answered, "Everyone is the age he has decided on, and I have decided to remain thirty."

This remarkably beautiful photo reflects Picasso's sense of showmanship and dramatic impact. He is truly a master at creating a mood. He does not seek, as he said, he finds. He follows his radiant Françoise lovingly and protectively, well behind her with the upraised umbrella. She walks freely, joyfully, but he moves forward like an erect Teutonic Knight. The wit, the showmanship, the composition, the originality, and especially the joy—all are impressive. Picasso is consistent in his life with his approach to art; he takes whatever elements are at hand—the umbrella, Françoise, himself—and with the aid of the photographer, he creates a stunningly beautiful and unforgettable picture.

Keeping in mind the recent, much-publicized explosions between this famous couple, what does this photo tell us about the Burtons' relationship?

On first impression, we are confronted with their grim, unhappy, possibly hostile faces. But can we detect the reasons for their looks? Are they simply physically exhausted? Are they unhappy with each other? Have they had one of their celebrated fights? If we saw no more, we might indeed think so, but let's look at the photo again.

The first photo was cropped to exclude their security escort, but here it is restored to its original condition. Look again, and you will have a completely different impression of what is going on. Although movie stars are conditioned to live virtually with cameras snapping in their faces, they are after all private beings and there are times when they want to be left alone. I think that's what is happening here. We see the guard trying, with outstretched hand, to shield them from the photographers, and we see the expressions of obvious distress on their faces. So my conclusion is that they are reacting more to the external photographic assault than to any personal upset. It is interesting to note that this photo was taken upon their arrival at Rome's Leonardo da Vinci airport, and the Italian *paparazzi* have been known to drive many dignitaries up the wall with their photographic snooping.

The real point is that we must guard against taking photos at their face value, since an alteration will yield quite different meanings.

These photos of Pat and Bill Loud were taken from the
footage of *An American Family,* the highly praised public
television documentary series that focused on the lives of
the Louds and their children. The contrast in personality
and emotional expression of the couple is jolting.

Examine their faces closely. What do you see?

For starters, he is the extrovert and she the introvert.
His mouth is wide open; hers sealed. His eyes are free;
hers behind sunglasses. He seems impulsive, she the
symbol of control. His happiness seems almost
excessive; her sad, drawn, depressed face indicates that
what is troubling her goes very deep. He copes with
light-hearted participation, while she appears to be
suffering stoically, repressing her true feelings.

The thing that impresses me about these two stills is
that they reflect, as much as any single still photo
possibly could, the totality of Pat and Bill Loud's
personalities as they emerged in the series. If you
watched the series, try to remember the personality traits
that struck you the most; then look at the photos again
and see if they confirm what you recall. I'm betting they
will.

This famous photo was used in the Army-McCarthy hearings—and cropped along the indicated lines—to prove the closeness between Private David Schine and Army Secretary Robert Stevens. Prior to his induction into the service, Schine had been on McCarthy's staff. First McCarthy tried to prevent Schine's induction, and then he and his staff made persistent efforts to obtain special consideration for Schine, which was not forthcoming. This infuriated McCarthy and his staff; in retaliation against Stevens, during the hearings the cropped photo was introduced as documentary evidence that Stevens was being especially nice and considerate to Schine in order to dissuade Senator McCarthy from continuing his investigation of the army.

The following day, lawyer Joseph Welch made a dramatic impact on the millions of people watching the hearing on television when he produced a copy of the original and complete photograph, which also included Air Force Colonel Jack T. Bradley and McCarthy's aide Frank Carr.

The whole exchange was a dramatic example of the power of photographic evidence, both when abused and when used properly. But let's speculate that the cropped version was all that existed, that indeed there were no other people present. With photoanalysis, how would we confront Senator McCarthy? In the photo, Private Schine is clearly beaming toward Army Secretary Stevens, a beam just as clearly not returned. It's even questionable whether Stevens is looking directly at Schine. In other words, that they were photographed together proves absolutely nothing, and certainly gives no evidence of any special relationship. Thus, the content of the photo indicates that McCarthy's charge of a special relationship was the utter hogwash it was later proven to be.

Examine closely this photo of eight men in uniform. That the occasion is not happy is immediately evident, but is there anything about these men that jolts you . . . something that makes you feel that this is far from a typical group photo of military men? Something inconsistent with the formality of a group photo?

Look at their hands, expecially the fingers of the sitting men. Do you see a non-verbal message? What unusual circumstances would cause them to resort to such communication?

Three of the men are giving the vulgar "up yours" finger sign with varying degrees of commitment and openness—from the bold, direct expression of the man on the extreme right to the more disguised, hesitant gesture of the man on the extreme left. The degree of commitment to their act also matches their facial expressions.

Now, we could certainly imagine that a group portrait of military men might give us a display like this, but normally it would be done in fun and jest. These men aren't having fun; they're restrained by something. Some faces reflect fright; others defiance; others uneasiness. Nonetheless, they want their message to get through, and it does—to anyone who can recognize it.

This is part of the *Pueblo* crew, captured by the North Koreans. This photo, taken by the North Koreans, was sent to an uncle of the man standing on the right. The men were prisoners, and their finger communication was an act of defiance that was successful in not being censored by their captors. Because of cultural differences—the North Koreans didn't understand the significance of the finger gestures—their message was not censored. To anyone who could interpret it, it said: "We are prisoners, but we are unbowed; we not only will not give in, we'll make fools of the North Koreans." They were later severely beaten when their guards learned what they had done, but by then their point had reached the world.

When Winston Churchill was elected Prime Minister in 1940, England was on the verge of collapse. But Churchill rallied his people with his iron will and unsurpassed eloquence: "You ask, what is our aim? I can answer in one word: Victory—victory at all costs, victory in spite of all terror, victory, however long and hard the road may be. . . ."

He came to power as his country's leader at sixty-five—the age of compulsory retirement in most organizations. He had already experienced his fair share of success and failure as a soldier, writer, and politician. His war-time speeches ignited his people, giving them hope and courage because he so passionately believed in Britain's ultimate victory.

Thousands of photographs of Churchill exist, and because he was so talented and famous, we could select endless themes about his growth and relationships with others. I have selected a series that reflects the relationship he had with his wife. Although these photos don't say everything about their personal relationship, they do reveal a significant aspect of it.

Churchill married Clementine Hozier in 1908 and, in his own words, "lived happily ever afterwards." All through their life together, Clementine was at his side, and we can see in the photos that she rarely looked at the camera, but almost always at her husband.

I will deal with the photographs separately, but before reading my explanations and conclusions, try analyzing the photos yourself, first singly, then collectively, and compare your analysis with mine.

The first photo **shows** the four-year-old Winston with his mother. She **gazes** attentively down at her son while he looks toward **the** camera. Although she could have sat in the chair **and** held him, she instead helps him balance on the chair, affirming his sense of independence, while still maintaining a firm, enveloping grip on his hands and drawing him to her. She appears attentive, but shows no signs of joy.

Six years after his marriage to Clementine, Churchill became First Lord of the Admiralty. He is now forty years old and out for a walk with his wife. She looks proudly at him as he walks forward and gazes directly at the photographer. It is clear that her world centers on him. Notice that she supports his left hand with her right arm rather than the more typical reversal—where the man offers the woman support with *his* arm.

Here Clementine stoops to pick up a glove Churchill has dropped as they arrive at the French Embassy to attend a dinner given by President Lebrun of France just prior to World War II. This photo would be less significant if she had stooped to pick up her own glove, but she's picking up *his.* He watches, making not the slightest effort to retrieve it himself, as if he expects her to do this for him.

288

The next photo depicts a most happy occasion for the Churchills, in America for a visit after World War II. Again Clementine's eyes are centered on him, as he engages in lively repartee during a press conference. She obviously is pleased with his spontaneous participation, and takes pleasure from his happiness.

Here Churchill is about to celebrate his seventy-third birthday. He looks pleased, happy, but it is Clementine who has made the move for physical contact, not even allowing his cigar to stop her from holding him.

In the above photo, the Churchills have returned from a holiday in France. He is recovering from a chill he contracted while swimming on the French Riviera. Again his wife makes the supportive contact by taking his elbow in her right hand as they walk from the airfield. We notice her nurselike concern as she centers visually on him.

At age seventy-seven, after being out of office for years, Churchill campaigns for reelection to become Prime Minister for a second term. He gives his classic "V for victory" sign as Clementine looks out the window, not at the public, but—as usual—at him, with her typical devotion, and with complete disregard for the camera.

   Lady Churchill literally breaks a path for her husband in
the photo above as they leave London's Royal Albert
Hall. Churchill is now in his early eighties, and now,
more than ever, his wife takes on the protective and
supportive role.

Posing for his eighty-fifth-birthday picture, Lady Churchill playfully prods her husband with her left hand as she attempts to cheer him out of his depression, but he seems unresponsive. He is tired and worn out from his losing battle for survival. For years he has been aware of his declining resources and energy brought on by aging and the strokes suffered when he returned to office in 1951.

This photo is one of the most moving, most touching photos I have ever experienced. Churchill has come to the window of his home to greet a crowd gathered to celebrate his ninetieth birthday. He is overcome with emotion at the public display on his behalf. Lady Churchill also seems overcome, but as usual her attention, her love, and her support center on him.

In this last photo, Lady Churchill unveils a bust of the late Prime Minister. She still centers her gaze on the symbol of her husband, even in death, as she had all through their over fifty years of married life.

How do we explain Churchill's unusual dependence and reliance on his wife? He was certainly not a helpless man, either emotionally or physically; but quite the opposite, a tower of strength and independence. In fact he played polo until he was fifty, and still rode to the hounds in his seventies. Nor does the source of his dependency seem to stem from his parents, who, in the usual manner of the upper class, were able to hire nurses for his care. Churchill wrote of his mother, "My mother shone for me like the Evening Star—I loved her dearly but at a distance." And of his father he said, "If I ever began to show the slightest idea of comradeship, he was immediately offended."

No, his dependency didn't come from his parents, but from his first nurse, Mrs. Everest, whom he described as "my confidante." For years he was sustained by her love, for he was really close to her, and when he was too old to need a nurse, she continued to share his secrets as his housekeeper. Throughout her life, she adored him and took care of him. When he learned that she was dying, he hurried to be with her, but when he arrived she was more concerned about his being soaked from the rain than about her own terminal illness.

Given that background, it is only natural that Churchill expected any woman in his life to be there always, to look at him, to adore him, to break his way through crowds, to prod him, to support him. And it was this relationship that he had with his wife, reflected in this series of photographs.

11.

Try your own photoanalysis

Using what you have learned about photoanalysis and its potential in the previous chapters, here is a chance to examine some photos entirely on your own—paying particular attention to body position, gestures, eyes, hands, and total facial expression, and what they indicate about interpersonal messages. Think about the people in the photos both as separate individuals and as individuals in communication. Look for tension and relaxation, harmony and conflict, all of the elements of the emotions, personality, and interpersonal relationships that have been discussed in this book.

Pinpoint those themes—based on what is happening in the photos—that you are fairly sure of; probe deeper into those themes about which you are doubtful or feel you have less of a reality base; look into all corners of the picture for possible extra clues.

You are now on your own, with the skills you have learned and with the visual sensitivity you have gained. Some photos are more ambiguous than others; all tell something significant. The more you linger with a particular photo, the more you may discover.

Although my own reactions to the photos can be found starting on page 311, you should formulate your own opinions before checking them against mine.

I quoted Lawrence Durrell's description of Georg Groddeck in the beginning of this book, and I repeat that now:

"I am not inviting you to follow me,
but to follow yourself.
I am only here to help if you need me."

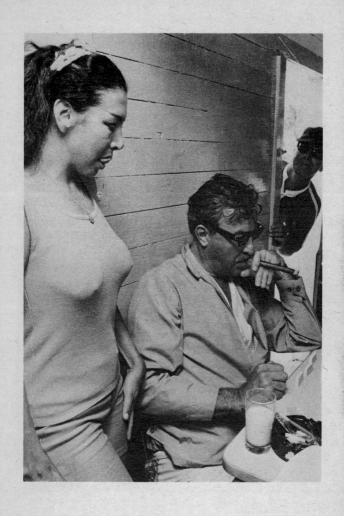

307

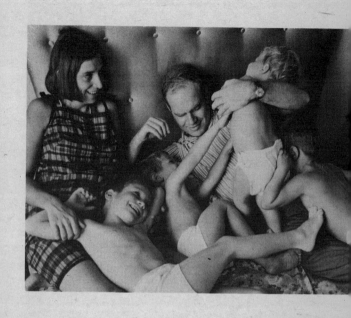

COMMENTS ON PHOTOGRAPHS
IN CHAPTER 11

Page 301

This is an ideal projective photo. There is such ambiguity and openendedness that one can read many things into it. This boy has just turned to face the photographer; his feet still point in the direction he was previously looking. But his facial expression is an enigma. What is he experiencing? Feeling? What are his thoughts? He appears shy, self-contained, and not about to give any clues to his emotions.

Now imagine that this boy begins to speak. What does he say? What would you say to him? And if he begins to walk, where would you have him go? The railroad tracks and freight cars are rich symbols for fantasy adventures. One can readily make up a story on this boy's past, present and future. Try it yourself. What you say may not only surprise you but also be personally and psychologically revealing.

Page 302

This is a revealing study in diplomatic communication that captures some significant dimensions of ease and difficulty as the three world leaders meet at a crucial point in World War II. It is obvious who the allies are, and who is apart.

Stalin sits erect, firm, uniformed and posed. His gaze centers neither on the camera nor on his companions.

He is sealed off, and self-absorbed. One can sense in his crossed fingers and crossed feet his defensiveness and self-protectiveness. He is determined not to respond, not to acknowledge the presence of Roosevelt or Churchill as they attempt visually to break through his self-imposed barrier. Yet his slightly bemused, knowing smile also suggests, even though he takes a defensive stance, that he is well able to cope with the existing situation, with whatever dfficulties crop up. It is the Big Three meeting in Teheran, Iran, and it's December, 1943.

Roosevelt occupies the central seat, the place of honor. He deliberately attempts to make visual contact with Stalin, as if to defrost him, to relax him. His left arm on the chair's arm rest actually touches Churchill at the elbow and signifies his closeness with Churchill. At the same time, we can see a degree of internal tension in Roosevelt in the way his fingers are curled into his hands rather than extended.

Churchill is the most comfortable and relaxed. His hat is off, hands, fingers and feet relaxed. He also makes an effort to reach Stalin visually. He has a welcoming smile, and he has selected the most comfortable, cushiony chair to sit in, contrasting significantly with Stalin sitting on hard wood.

The photo is a good example of consistency. All parts of each body, their attitudes and positioning tell the same story about who is open, who is relaxed, and the direction of the interpersonal communication. These are three men who know exactly who they are, and express their personalities as well with their bodies as with their words.

Page 303

In this photo, the act of exposure is obvious. The woman at your right is singling out another woman with what looks like very exaggerated rage and fierce contempt. In spite of the force of the look and gesture, the woman with bowed head cannot face her accuser. But she is deeply affected and attempts to remain in control of herself. Notice the fist she makes with her right hand.

Most of the other people focus on the action and center on the accused, but their eyes lack the contempt of the accusing woman. They simply look on curiously, as if watching a similar scene in a play. The official sitting at the desk stares blankly ahead of him, avoiding the heated transaction and showing no emotion. His pen is more a prop than functional, for he has written nothing on his pad.

Two bits of information give clues to the setting and circumstances of this photo. The great range of clothing— from uniforms to concentration camp pajamas—and the documents—passports or some kind of identification papers—suggest this might be a camp for refugees or displaced persons.

In fact, the photo was taken at a camp for displaced persons in Dessau, Germany, in 1945. The people are waiting for repatriation. The accused woman is a Gestapo informer who was exposed as she attempted to mingle with the other refugees in order to be released.

Page 304

It doesn't take much information—or photoanalysis—to realize that this setting must be a day room in some sort of hospital or institution. But what kind of place is it, with what kind of patients? The animal designs on the wall, the withdrawn, vacant and isolated look on each patient's face, their ragged, skimpy clothing and the bare feet strongly suggest either that they are chronically regressed in a state mental hospital or are inpatients at a state hospital for the mentally retarded.

These people are so centered within themselves that however limited the gesture, it is genuinely moving to see that the man at the left has reached out to make contact with his neighbor. The center figure raises his arm toward his face, as if annoyed with or startled by the outside intrusion; but he makes no effort to acknowledge it. Notice that neither man is able to make visual contact with the other. It is also significant that the man on the left reaches forward while he attempts at the same time to remain in his chair. It would have been easier to touch the other man if he had moved closer, but he needed to remain securely anchored. His efforts to communicate may be related to the paper he holds in his right hand. Perhaps he wishes to show it to his neighbor.

The man standing in the doorway is from another world. The look on his face reflects disgust. But is his look due to revulsion toward the patients or toward the miserable conditions of the hospital? Judging from his dress and participation, he does not appear to be visitor, doctor or attendant. He stands as if he is showing the place off to someone.

In fact, the man is New York Congressman Mario Biaggi at Willowbrook Hospital in early 1972. He had invited news photographers to accompany him on his tour of the state hospital for retardation in order to more effectively expose the scandalous conditions there.

Page 305

You're looking at a three-way study in unacknowledged communication. The cigar smoker, central in this scene, gazes intently at the five upright rectangular blocks on the table, probably dominoes. He is so engrossed in the game that he's oblivious to the surrounding activity and unaffected by outside vibrations.

A sexually provocative lady in shorts stands at his side. What amuses me is her erotic posturing—her tongue protruding to her upper lip and her left hand deliberately feeling her thigh—which is so inconsistent with what is going on. She retains her sexuality even at dominoes!

Although the cigar smoker does not acknowledge the

314

woman's presence with either gesture or look, her participation is not wasted. The man peering through the door fully appreciates what he sees. I feel his appearance on the scene is accidental, and the sexy woman does not notice his intrusion. Most likely the domino player has created this scene, using the woman as a prop. He has surrounded himself with symbols—drink, cigar, sex, free play time—to communicate a leisurely style of living.

My view is to a great extent confirmed when we identify the man as the now-deceased, former Harlem Congressman, Adam Clayton Powell. The photo was taken one day after the New York Court of Appeals threw out monetary claims against him stemming from a lengthy battle with a Harlem widow he defamed.

Page 306

Some photos say it all! Words are not needed to further clarify a scene because there are no hidden or obscure elements. This is such a photo. Here, a grief-stricken boy looks to his dog for love and support. An obviously sympathetic woman attempts to comfort the boy, but he wants his dog, suggesting that the woman is not that close to him. The way he encloses his body protectively and nuzzles up to the dog suggests his loss is grave and that most likely he will be mourning for some time.

We are moved by the photo, but its impact is heightened when we are told that this boy has just seen his father shoot and kill his mother.

Page 307

This is a family of three, but on first impression the mother seems almost peripheral, like a prop. The emotional intimacy and communication is clearly between daughter and father. Margaret adores her father and he returns the adoration. Truman has gathered his girl to him with a fleshy right hand grip on her hip. He is not afraid to be physical. But his encompassing hold has thrown her slightly off balance as she leans against his body, and she uses her own hands and forearms on his thigh for support as well as contact. One could be misled that her touch is erotic, but if you look at her body balance, you will realize there is nowhere else she could have placed her hands.

The photo indicates a physical ease within the family. It is okay to touch, something unfortunately missing in too many families. Father and daughter have the close contact, both physically and visually, while Bess looks wistful, forlorn, left out, almost disapproving. She focuses neither on the father-daughter exchange nor the photographer. Her mouth, fingers, and legs are all sealed. In this photo, she appears a closed, self-contained entity. Notice the contrasting leg positionings. Father and daughter have their legs open (and they are open to each other), while the closed legs of the mother conforms with her closed presence. Their heads reveal the same story.

Truman almost surely spoiled Margaret at that age, while Bess was more rational, responsible, controlling, and disapproving. But she is not left out in the cold completely. You can see that Truman has also gathered her to him with his left hand, two of his fingers coming around her waist.

This photo is an excellent, dynamic example of how photos can capture significant interfamily relationships.

Page 308

Here's an unusual sight; yet it's refreshing to see these dancing women in various states of undress, depending on how they feel about their bodies and being photographed.

The occasion is joyous. There is a sense of life, abandonment and spontaneity that contrasts sharply with the stark background of dead trees, reminders of a past forest fire. All the women are barefoot and move to some form of music or rhythm.

As we look closer, we realize that many are actually paired in their dancing. The two women on the left (one carrying her child) are swinging each other with locked elbows; the woman in the middle (facing the camera) claps a rhythmical beat to the girl with her back to the photographer; and the two women on the right are also swinging each other. The youngster at the right wants a partner also. We can almost hear her say, "Me, too, I wanna dance, too."

There is an all-pervading sense of enjoyment.

Page 309

The photo of this delightful couple reveals delicious laughter on the woman's part. She is really cracking up, and her facial expression reflects a healthy mix of humor and pleasure. The man has the sheepish look of someone caught in an embarrassing moment. But what's it all about?

The photo tells the story. The drying tobacco leaves that hang overhead and the couple's dress suggest they are tobacco farmers. Their easy closeness indicates they are probably married. The degree of her laughter and her arms at her sides point to her as the observer, while his face, his arms, and especially his hands, give the telling clue. His stance would be a most unusual way to pose for a photo. His hands have a purpose, as we can see that his fingers are holding up his pants, which appear too loose and unsupported by his belt. The photo was most likely taken the moment after he realized that his pants were slipping, and her bursting laughter exploded.

That is in fact the case. The photographer has just told the man that his pants are falling down, and the photo captures his look of having been caught in an embarrassing yet humorous experience.

Page 310

This is a joyous scene, with bodies interwoven everywhere. Energy flows from this photo, and this family. There is physical freedom to romp, touch, relate, and the photo captures such spontaneity that the photographer must also be a close friend, for I doubt that any family would show such intimacy otherwise. It is the kind of photo that one can too easily dismiss as a "happy shot," without further scrutiny. But as in all photos, this one has its story to tell.

The romping is more than simple fun. There is also a lively and healthy mix of sibling rivalry and rough-housing, focused on who will be central and closest to Daddy. Such rivalry is especially keen when the siblings are all close in age, when no single brother gets a chance to be the special "baby" for too long.

Focus with me on the participation of each brother. The youngest is readily identifiable. He stands in diapers, with safety pin, making an all-out effort to be closest to Daddy. Although reinforced by his father's left arm, he has trouble making headway because of the strong arm tactics of his second youngest brother(pushing at him from the left) and another brother who attempts to pull him away with a hip grip.

The second youngest brother is in a key position, between both parents, on his back and nestled under his father's right arm. He battles to maintain this position, which is threatened by the youngest brother. The third youngest struggles forward and upward on his father's legs, trying to dig a place for himself.

The oldest brother appears the most independent. He is closer to his mother, who gently restrains his right arm, but not his right foot, which he uses playfully to restrain one brother from gaining ground.

All this rivalry is part of growing developmentally in a family, and certainly is not always fun and games.

The father has the place of honor; he is the wanted one. He may have just come home from work, which would

318

explain why such lavish attention is being heaped on him. The fact that all the boys are in their shorts suggests that it's either bedtime or very hot. The mother thoroughly enjoys the scene and centers her attention on her youngest's struggles.

These brothers may well be a handful in other circumstances. The father gives some clues as to how he copes: making no effort to stop the two youngest or interfere with their struggle. He supports the youngest with his arm (to make the struggle an even match?), and leaves his right arm free for the moment, hovering over the second youngest's head. And he shows a tickled, amused look as he watches the action swirling around.

Your Inner Child of the Past

🏵 Once you were a child.

🏵 That child still lives within you—influencing and interfering in your adult life.

🏵 This book tells you HOW TO SOLVE YOUR ADULT EMOTIONAL PROBLEMS by recognizing, accepting and managing the feelings of YOUR INNER CHILD OF THE PAST.

BY W. HUGH MISSILDINE, M.D.

AMONG THE NEW IDEAS AND FRESH APPROACHES IN THIS BOOK ARE:

- There are four people in every marriage bed
- Every "lone wolf" has an unwelcome companion
- There are times when it's all wrong to try to "do better"
- How the "command-resistance" cycle of childhood leads to adult sexual frustration
- How to be the right kind of parent to your "inner child of the past"
- Six rules for happy family life

▼ AT YOUR BOOKSTORE OR MAIL THIS COUPON NOW FOR FREE 30-DAY TRIAL ▼

SIMON AND SCHUSTER ● DEPT. S-45
630 Fifth Avenue, New York, N.Y. 10020

Please send me a copy of YOUR INNER CHILD OF THE PAST. I must be completely satisfied with the book or I may return it within 30 days and owe nothing. Otherwise I will send $7.95 plus mailing costs, as payment in full.

Name ....

Address ....

City .... State .... Zip ....

☐ SAVE POSTAGE. Check here if you enclose check or money order for $7.95 as payment in full—then we pay postage. Same 30-day privilege guarantee holds. N.Y. residents please add applicable sales tax.

P 68/2

A NATIONAL BESTSELLER AT $12.95 –NOW ONLY $4.95

Through the economies of paperback publishing, THE JOY OF SEX is now available in the same large format as the $12.95 hardbound book, complete and unabridged, with all the original full-color illustrations—at only $4.95!

The Gourmet Guide to Love Making for men and women who are familiar with the basics — and want to go on from there

THE NATIONAL BESTSELLER AT $12.95 NOW $4.95

The Joy of Sex
A Gourmet Guide to Love Making

COMPLETE AND UNABRIDGED ILLUSTRATED EDITION

EDITED BY ALEX COMFORT, M.B., Ph.D.

SIMON AND SCHUSTER,   **Dept. 912**
630 Fifth Ave., New York, N.Y. 10020

Please send me THE JOY OF SEX as checked below, for which I enclose payment as indicated (New York residents please add applicable sales tax). For sale to adults over 21 only. If not completely satisfied, I may return book(s) postpaid within 14 days for complete refund.

_____copy(ies) paperbound edition @ $4.95
_____copy(ies) hardbound edition @ $12.95

Check or money order for $_____ is enclosed.

Name_____

Address_____

City_____State_____Zip_____

S 96/6

IF YOU ENJOYED

Photoanalysis

YOU'LL WANT TO READ
MORE OF THESE BEST-SELLING GUIDES
TO UNDERSTANDING OTHER PEOPLE

BODY LANGUAGE

The physical signals we all send out—from crossing legs to folding arms—are analyzed to show how we can read and understand body movements.

THE LÜSCHER COLOR TEST

Tells you how revealing color choices can be. A simple, remarkable test that can help you discover hidden personality traits!

HOW TO READ A PERSON LIKE A BOOK

An invaluable key to the silent language of hidden thoughts, it describes the nonverbal language of our bodies and how it conveys more about what we *really* mean than words could ever say!

META-TALK

The newest paperback book by the authors of HOW TO READ A PERSON LIKE A BOOK, META-TALK is a fascinating and completely innovative guide to hidden meanings in conversation.

▼ **AT YOUR BOOKSTORE OR MAIL THE COUPON BELOW** ▼

Mail Service Department   **POCKET BOOKS**   Dept. PH-1
A Division of Simon & Schuster, Inc.,
1 West 39th Street, New York, New York 10018
Please send me the following:

QUAN-TITY	NO.	TITLE		AMOUNT
....	78827	THE LÜSCHER COLOR TEST	$1.95	....
....	78524	BODY LANGUAGE	$1.50	....
....	78593	HOW TO READ A PERSON		
		LIKE A BOOK	$1.50	....
....	78879	META-TALK	$1.50	....
		MAILING AND HANDLING CHARGE—25¢		....
		(50¢ for 2 or more copies)		
		TOTAL		....

Please enclose check or money order.

We are not responsible for orders containing cash.
(Please print clearly)

NAME _____

ADDRESS_____

CITY_____ STATE_____ ZIP_____

P104/5